ALL BALLS AND ASHES

A comedy by

Mark Robberts

Published by Playstage
United Kingdom

An imprint of Write Publications Ltd

www.playsforadults.com

Designed by Kate Lowe, Greensands Graphics
Printed by Creeds Ltd, Bridport, Dorset

NOTE FROM THE AUTHOR

This play was originally written as a TV pilot when the BBC was looking to replace *Last of the Summer Wine*, at which time it would have been directed by the, then, producer, Gareth Gwenlan. Following public outcry, *LOTSW*, was retained and the pilot would have continued to gather dust on the BBC shelves, had I not reclaimed and rewritten it with the title *All Balls and Ashes*. Following the premiere, it was nominated for a comedy of the year award but lost out to a Derek Benfield play.

As I am always mindful of the minimalist preferences for stage productions in both size and stage furniture, I did initially have some concerns for this play. However, it has been pleasing to note the ingenuity of set designers. And, at each staging, the feedback from the casts has been overwhelmingly positive. 'An enjoyable, fun play' seems to be the general opinion.

One of the key elements is the sound offstage of a chamber pot being struck by Eli's steel helmet. Here, it was realised – after much intriguing research – that only a genuine, good quality chamber pot would produce the right note!

Mark Robberts

Note to producers about staging "All Balls and Ashes"

There is a large amount of physical comedy in this play – which needs to be almost pantomimic in execution.

The trio of FRANK, ELI and GEORGE, particularly during Act I, Scene 5; Act II, Scene 1; and Act II, Scene 5, are in full-on clown mode and, as such, movements should be exaggerated. The VICAR also joins in with this slapstick.

The VICAR and POTTS also have a clown-like moment in Act II, Scene 5 – involving a shotgun and a telescope, which requires careful choreography.

The most difficult verbal comedy is executed by the two wives – VERA and DOLLY – in Act I, Scene 4, because they have to finish each other's sentences. This must be seamless and requires a great deal of practice to achieve precision.

It almost goes without saying that the pace, as with all good farces, should rattle along. However, it should not be at the expense of the comedic but contemplative moments in The Cloggers Arms.

THE CHARACTERS

FRANK	the 'mastermind' of the three idiots central to the plot.
ELI	completely daft.
GEORGE	a reasonably responsible individual but easily led.
MARY	a 'no nonsense' Yorkshire lass with a soft heart.
FREDA	an out-and-out dragon. Go for it!
DAWSON	a dozy village policeman. Gullible.
VICAR	a slightly vague clergyman reliant on his hip flask. Also gullible.
POTTS	a very pompous individual.
MARIGOLD	very flirty. A middle-aged 'airhead'.
VERA & DOLLY	joined at the hip. Think alike, finish each other's sentences. Very possible that they dress alike too.

THE SETS

This play requires set changes, which some groups may find difficult on a small stage. However, we have devised some suggested scenery plans at the back of the book, that may solve various problems.

Note: for all scenes in The Clogger's Arms, we would suggest that all 'pints of beer' are ready-poured under the bar, as with any other drinks. It would be too much to expect any drama group to organise working beer pumps!

MUSIC

Between scenes, we would suggest Morris Dance or brass band music – something light and in keeping with the premise of the play.

SOUND EFFECTS

As the author has stated, the steel helmet against a chamberpot really works best done manually with the real objects! Similarly, the sound effect of bolts being drawn on the doors of The Cloggers Arms is best done offstage with a couple of heavy bolts affixed to a piece of wood. Owl hoots can be downloaded from the internet from a site like www.sound-effects-library.com

FREDA's BEDROOM SCENE

You will see from the script that this requires sound effects (snoring, a scream, helmet against china etc.) For best effect these should all be done by someone standing behind the scenery. Similarly, when the script calls for the bedroom light to come on in the upstairs window, the least complicated way of doing this is to have someone standing behind the flat with a battery operated lamp that can be switched on and off.

ALL BALLS AND ASHES

CAST *(In order of appearance)*

MARY	Barmaid at the Cloggers pub. Aged 35–45.
FRANK BOTTOMLEY	Former cricketer. In his early 60s.
GEORGE	Landlord of the Cloggers In his 50s.
ELI	Captains the cricket team on charity days. In his 60s.
FREDA	Seth's widow, basically a dragon in feminine guise in her late 60s.
ALF DAWSON	Local police sergeant. Mid 40s.
VICAR.	Algernon Makepeace. In his 50s.
ARNOLD POTTS	Pompous local bank manager, in his 50s.
MARIGOLD POTTS	Wife of Arnold, a sexy little creature, in her 50s.
VERA BOTTOMLEY	Wife of Frank. In her early 60s.
DOLLY	Wife of Eli, in her 60s.

6 men and 5 women.

The action takes place in various locations in and around the village of Greenbridge on the Yorkshire/Lancashire borders.

ALL BALLS AND ASHES

ACT 1.

Scene 1.

The "snug" of The Cloggers Arms. There is a bar, with optics etc. behind and pumps on the bar itself. To the side and in front of the bar is a table with three chairs. A poster is on the wall for a forthcoming charity cricket match. FRANK is sitting alone at the table, nursing a pint of beer and toying with some dominoes.

GEORGE is behind the bar reading a racing paper. MARY is wiping the top of the bar and eyeing FRANK with suspicion.

MARY — I've heard of your sort Frank Bottomley. Memorising the backs of them dominoes so's you'll now what your mates are holding…

FRANK — It's just a quiet bit of manly idling. A chap's entitled to a bit of quiet, manly idling.

MARY — Seems to me you and your lot are specialists at idling.

GEORGE — So, where are your mates, Frank. Bit late aren't they?

FRANK — Don't you fret, George. They'll be along shortly, they won't miss the team selection for the charity match.

MARY — This team selection. I suppose it'll be in need of, shall we say… liquid lubrication.

FRANK — Of course. That's the secret ingredient when it comes to the important projects in life. Get that right and job's a good un.

Did you know it were liquid lubrication that helped the Egyptians build the pyramids?

MARY Just as well then that you weren't on that job. There'd be more supping than building.

GEORGE And no ruddy pyramids.

FRANK Oh, there'd be pyramids all right.

GEORGE But not the right shape, eh?

FRANK Maybe, but then cricket's different. You see George, it's all a matter of – balance – fine tuning and a few nights practice.

GEORGE I always thought it was about daft pillocks running between them sticks, and pretending they're not past it. Present company excepted, of course.

FRANK Those sticks are wickets, made of stout English ash, George. But it's really all down to practise...

MARY Practise, eh? Do you meaning cricket or supping.

FRANK Don't you start, it's bad enough with him behind the bar.

GEORGE You reckon you'll be ready? I mean, you're leaving it a bit late, there's only a couple of weeks to go....

FRANK No problem. Once we've put on our whites and the lads get hold of a ball, it'll all come flooding back. The fours *(FRANK signals a four)* The sixes *(He signals a six)* Bowling their opening bat all ends up... *(Bowls an imaginary ball then winces and clutches his arm in pain)... (ELI enters with a glazed expression. He seems agitated and keeps repeatedly twisting his cap in his hands.)*

MARY Well, speak of the devil. Here's one of your mates now. Usual, Eli?

(ELI ignores her and walks straight past the bar.)

FRANK Hey up! That's a first. He's missed the bar. Poor lad's either sick or lost his memory....

GEORGE As long as he hasn't forgotten how much he owes on the slate. Pull him a pint Mary, that'll put him right....

ELI *(dramatic)* A pint? A pint? It'll take more than a pint to put me right. I need a minute or two to compose myself.

GEORGE You look as though you're decomposing if you ask me, lad...

ELI That's not funny, George. If you were not the landlord I'd lamp your ear–hole...

GEORGE Now steady on, lad. I only said...

ELI I heard, George. You've got a mouth like a parish over. NOW SHUT IT!

FRANK Steady on, lad. Not like you to take on so, Eli. Whatever's troubling you, you'd best cough it up. You're wasting good drinking time. Maybe you'll feel better with a pint inside you.

ELI Never mind the beer – it's Seth....

MARY SETH! What about Seth?

GEORGE Whatever it is, no doubt Seth will tell us himself. I'll put one up for him.

ELI You mean – you haven't heard?

MARY Heard! Heard what, Eli?

ELI Put it this way. I shouldn't bother pulling that pint. He'll not want it. The poor lad's supped his last...

GEORGE You don't mean – the daft beggar's gone – TEETOTAL? *(Pause)* A fat lot of good that'll do for my trade...

ELI — No, he hasn't gone teetotal. Fact is – he's done something far worse. Like falling off his perch…

MARY — Oh, the poor lad. I hope he hasn't hurt himself. Maybe he'll want a whisky when he comes…

GEORGE — I don't think a whisky will do much good, Mary. If I'm not mistaken what Eli means is, Seth has passed on.

(MARY goes rigid with shock.)

ELI — Got it in one, George.

FRANK — The poor lad. He was playing dominoes here just last night and winning too. Nearly bankrupted me. Took nigh on 50p from me…

ELI — I shouldn't bet on getting it back….

GEORGE — Imagine, Seth popping his clogs….

ELI — Aye, cocked up his toes. Stiff as a board…

(As they reverently stand and remove their caps, there is a deep moan from MARY and she drops the empty glass she was holding.)

GEORGE — Hey! Steady on lass, that's money you're dropping there… *(GEORGE hastily rummages behind the bar and produces a notebook)* By the heck, Seth owed nigh on £5 on the slate. I'll be ruined if any more of you pop off. Here, Mary, pour me a whisky – a double –and quick…

(MARY doesn't answer. She looks distressed.)

GEORGE — Mary! Are you – you alright?

MARY — Yes, I mean – No. It's the news – about Seth. So sudden. I'm not feeling good….

FRANK — Aye, we know how you feel, lass. Bit of a shock, eh? Poor devil, best pace bowler Greenbridge ever had. Took a few wickets did the old lad. There were a few left in him yet. What was he, seventy?

ELI Seventy two...

GEORGE Seventy two! You sure? Could have sworn he took more wickets than that.

ELI No, you daft pillock. He was seventy two years old. Only a spring chicken. Given out by the great umpire in the sky, *(ELI points up – all eyes follow his pointing finger)* just a few runs short of his century.

(MARY disappears and then returns carrying her coat. She is clearly upset.)

MARY Er, George. I – er – could I – could I?

GEORGE Pay for that glass? It's alright, lass, I'll let you off with that one...

MARY No, I'd like to go – I'm not feeling well. Could do with some fresh air. Could I?

GEORGE Aye, go on with you lass. Can't have you breaking glasses all night and crying in the customers beer....

(MARY exits.)

FRANK This business with Seth. Do we know what happened?

ELI Thought you'd have known, you living next door. His widow blames it on the cricket and all those practise nights.

FRANK Nay, I've spent most of today on the allotment. Practice nights? What practice nights?

ELI Well, we did talk about it – quite a lot in fact. You remember how excited he got? Anyway seems he got his kit out, put it on and was limbering up in the bedroom when the daft man bowled himself down the stairs, top to bottom and there he was, given out but like a true cricketer – still clutching the ball…

FRANK Poor beggar….

ELI The doctor said in all his forty years he'd never had a case like it. Reckons Seth made a fatal mistake, one so unique he felt obliged to put it on the death certificate and in the medical journal.

GEORGE Gerraway! And that was?

ELI He forgot to let go of the ball.

(There is a moment's silence as they reflect on the tragedy of this.)

FRANK Poor lad, given out before his innings is done. Like I allus said, dangerous game is cricket. A real man's game…

GEORGE Well, with a man short I suppose you'll be cancelling the match then.

FRANK Cancel! CANCEL! Nay, the match is for charity – and Seth now…

ELI A man short? What about you, George. I mean – you look as though you could be handy with a bat. Maybe stand in for Seth…

GEORGE Me! Stand in for Seth? Sorry lads but I'll be busy that day – Er, what day did you say it was?

FRANK Two weeks next Saturday…

GEORGE No, I'm sure that's the day I'll be busy. Sorry lads…

FRANK Then we'll have to manage without. Pity. All them lasses will be disappointed.

GEORGE Er, did you say – lasses?

ELI Aye. They were looking forward to the game as much as Seth. He had a way with the women. Never could understand why. He used to tell 'em his nickname was – Hot Balls Seth. *(Pause)* Mind you, he will be now – his widow says he's being cremated....

GEORGE Er, well, can't let the lasses down, I suppose? Perhaps I will be free that day...

FRANK Cremated, eh? Hey! You know what that means...ashes!

GEORGE What do you expect at a cremation?

FRANK No, it was something Seth said, at this very table as I live and breathe...

ELI *(excited)* Aye, I remember! He said, if anything happened to him, we were to have a pint on him. So, two pints of your best, landlord. We're drinking to Seth's memory and to hell with the consequences. I don't care if I do get drunk...

GEORGE Halves, lads?

ELI Halves, George!? They're for wimps. Make 'em pints.

FRANK I'll drink to that. But that wasn't what I meant. Eli said, he'd like his ashes scattered over Jasper's Bottom in memory of all the happy times he'd spent there.

ELI That's so, it's all coming back to me now.

GEORGE And that was it? He didn't want much did he?

FRANK Ah, not quite all, George. There was something else he asked for, something special.

GEORGE That's what I'd like, something special. With a couple of strippers to see me on my way.

ELI No, Seth wanted to go out in style...

GEORGE I'd call a couple of strippers going out in style. Might ask them to come with me.

FRANK *(irritated by GEORGE's singlemindedness)* It had nothing to do with strippers! Seth wanted – a brass band...

GEORGE A band?

FRANK Yes, a band, a proper band. Oh...and Morris Men.

GEORGE *(disbelieving)* You're making this up! Having me on...

ELI No, George. Seth wanted his ashes scattered on the cricket field, with a brass band playing and Morris Men dancing.

FRANK That's true, I remember that, and – we promised him we'd do it...

ELI Mind you, we were full of ale at the time. But then, a promise to a mate is a promise – and like as not we'll do the same for you when you go, George...

GEORGE I've got no immediate plans....

FRANK You know, he could have given us more warning. Won't be easy getting a band and Morris men at short notice.

GEORGE I take it you've spoken to Seth's widow and she's agreed to all this.

ELI Er, yes. I mean no.

GEORGE From what I know of that battleaxe, I wouldn't fancy telling her! She'll eat you up and spit you out before you can say "Brass Band."*(GEORGE goes to the bar and pulls the pints of beer.)*

FRANK George is right you know.

ELI *(insistent)* But Seth was a mate. One of the best. At the very least we ought to have a word.

(GEORGE returns carrying two pints)

GEORGE There you are, lads. Two pints of the best. Now who's paying?

ELI Good question, George. But these are on Seth and being as he's not here, you'd best put them on his slate. Oh, and have one yourself, eh?

GEORGE Good idea. Best offer I've had all night...

BLACKOUT.

MUSIC.

End of Scene 1.

ALL BALLS AND ASHES

ACT 1.

Scene 2.

As the lights come up, the setting is FREDA's living room. There is an armchair, a sofa and a side table, on which are Seth's ashes in an urn. FREDA is reading a newspaper. There is a tentative knock on the door. She ignores it.

FRANK *(offstage)* Maybe she didn't hear you. Give it some wellie, Eli.

(There is a louder knock.)

FREDA *(shouting)* Heard you the first time!! Not deaf you know. There's no need to batter the door down....*(Grumbling – she gets up and goes offstage to answer the door. She says the first sentence offstage)* Oh, it's you. Might have had second thoughts if I'd known. *(She enters followed by FRANK and ELI)* So what do you want at this time of night. Have you no respect – don't you know you're about to interrupt my favourite programme on telly?

ELI By heck, is it that late? Er, sorry to disturb you Freda, but we have something...

FREDA *(interrupting testily)* Something what?

FRANK To discuss – about – Seth...

FREDA About Seth?

(FRANK and ELI stand in uncomfortable silence. Each hoping the other will speak up first.)

Has gaining admission struck you dumb? You said you had summat to discuss. Mind you, if we get much beyond dominoes, beer and cricket, I shall be surprised... *(She opens the newspaper and spreads the sheets on settee)* You have two minutes. So, whilst we're waiting for you to remember what you came for, you might as well sit down.

(The pair sit and fidget in awkward silence.)

Well, are you going to sit there like two daft, dumb monkeys? The clock's ticking, so let me remind you. You said something about Seth. .That ring a bell?

FRANK Er, it was a nice funeral service, Freda.

ELI Yes, Seth had as warm send–off.

FREDA Of course he had a warm send–off. What do you expect at a cremation. But I'm sure you didn't come here to tell me that. I reckon you're after something... maybe something Seth left behind?

FRANK You're getting warm, Freda...

ELI *(trying to joke)* But not as warm as Seth, eh? *(A nudge from FRANK shuts ELI up.)*

FREDA If you're after his cricketing clothes, you're too late. He went to the crem in those.

ELI That was nice of the old lad. Thinking of his pals and cricket right to the end...

FREDA Seth thinking of the lads? Was he heck as like. The cricket clothes were my idea. Seemed a good way to get rid of them. Seth went wearing two lots – cap n'all. You should have seen the undertaker's face when I told him what I wanted...

FRANK By the cringe. The poor lad must have been warm wearing that lot...

ELI Wonder they got him in his box. But tell me Freda, if he went wearing his cricketing clobber, did you remember to take his beer money out of his back pocket?

FREDA *(annoyed)* Money! What money?

ELI Lad allus kept a fiver – in his back pocket for a pint or two after the game.

FRANK He called it his supping money.

FREDA Supping money? If this is a game in stupidity, you're winning hands down. So why don't you let me in on whatever it is you've really come about. If you've come for his balls – you're too late – they went with him...

ELI I should hope so. Whether he's playing at home or away, a cricketing man's no good without his balls...

FREDA What was that?

ELI I said – he were good – with his balls...

FRANK Then what about his cricket bat?

FREDA That went n'all. Woodworm...

ELI Woodworm?

FREDA Aye, there was more worm than bat. So, was there anything else?

FRANK Yes, but it's a little delicate, Freda...

FREDA Everything's delicate where you lot are concerned. But I'm feeling rather generous, so take advantage and let me be the judge of whether it's fit for human consumption.

ELI It was summat Seth said – about what he would like when he – cocked his toes up...

FRANK *(cutting in, hastily)* What Eli means is that Seth asked – in the way of last wishes you understand – the lads to perform a certain – ceremony

FREDA He asked that – before he passed away?

ELI It would have been difficult after he'd passed on....

FREDA A certain ceremony, you said.

FRANK Yes, and we just – wondered – if he'd discussed it – with you?

FREDA Seth! Discuss anything with me? Let me tell you, lately apart from his tools in the garden shed, co–op divi, his false teeth, lumbago and varicose veins, he ne'er discussed anything with me. Talking was the least of his priorities. But then I suppose for all his faults, he was faithful – to the end. Not like some other chaps I could mention. Give a man a chance to spread his wings, before you know where you are, he's a peacock displaying to all and sundry...

ELI So, he didn't talk about any – like – arrangements?

FREDA Well, there was one other thing...

FRANK and ELI. *(in unison)* Yes. And that was?

FREDA His piles. Lately, he kept going on about his piles. Reckoned the only way to get relief was to go out walking all hours....

ELI Funny, he never mentioned them to us. And there was nothing else?

FREDA Isn't that enough to be going on with?

ELI See Frank. I said he wouldn't have said owt. Best forget it. Sorry to have troubled you, Freda.

(They get up to leave.)

FREDA Oh, no you don't Eli Cruickshanks! Sit yourself down. You n'all, Frank Bottomley. You're not leaving until you tell me about this certain ceremony. More than likely it concerned a pint or two...

FRANK If you want to know...

FREDA *(cutting in)* And I do....

FRANK Truth is – it had nothing to do with supping...

FREDA That's strange for a start...

ELI It concerned – his – ashes. Seth said – when he went – like he did, he would like his ashes scattered – over...

FRANK Over...

FREDA Over?

ELI Over...

FREDA Go on...

FRANK *(weakly)* Jasper's – Bottom...

FREDA What did you say?

(FRANK and ELI cringe)

ELI It was what Seth wanted. To celebrate all the happy times he spent there. A nice, truly dignified ceremony...

FREDA And a dignified ceremony is what he got. Five minutes at the crem. So, are we done...

FRANK Er, not quite. There was a just a tiny bit more – like – Morris Men...

FREDA Morris Men? Doing what may I ask?

ELI What they normally do, dance, I suppose – waving hankies... *(ELI pulls out a hanky and weakly waves it about)*

FRANK And bells – to go with the hankies of course. Er, sorry Freda, I haven't got a bell...

FREDA Thank God for that. Thought for a moment I was going to get Big Bloody Ben!

ELI You haven't told her the best bit, Frank...

FREDA There's more? May the good Lord spare me...

FRANK Oh, yes. He wanted the job done right and proper. Said as how he'd like a brass band – playing...

ELI *(cutting in)* Like they do. Said he was thinking of you. Reckoned it would put a smile on your face...

(FREDA sits silent and stone–faced.)

FRANK Er, you're not smiling, Freda...

FREDA *(acidly)* Haven't you noticed. I'm in hysterics. Ashes, cricket field, Morris Men and now a brass band! By heck, Enid Blyton would have had a field day with you two. You must think I'm not a full shilling. Why, there's more twists in your minds than a game of pontoon.

FRANK Now don't take on so, Freda love!

FREDA Don't you love me, Frank Bottomley.!

ELI But it's all true, Freda...

FREDA Made up, I reckon. You've been to the Cloggers Arms a few times too many.

FRANK Then, does that mean – the answer's 'no'?

FREDA Got it in one, super–brain. I'm not having my Seth lying amongst wriggly worms, rabbit droppings and where those mucky cows have been. He's staying here in the warmth with me.

ELI Poor Seth. That's a right shame. He liked rabbits, worms too. Used to dig 'em up and feed them to the birds.

FRANK Oh, yes, like he always said, he liked his birds. Spent hours bird–watching...

FREDA Well, a few harmless pursuits doesn't do a man any harm....

ELI So, where is the old lad then?

(FREDA indicates the urn)

FREDA He sits there during the day; watches the telly with me. Loves Coronation Street. Come bedtime he goes upstairs with me. Has pride of place on the bedside cabinet and each night...

FRANK *(cutting in)* He can gaze at you. By the cringe....

FREDA And what's wrong with that, Frank Bottomley? I reckon when he was alive he only had eyes for me...

ELI Now every night he gets the full Monty...

FRANK With a ton of imagination – it could even sound – romantic...

FREDA *(standing up)* Well, I reckon I've given you enough of my time. So you'd best be off and take all your daft notions and silly ideas with you... *(FREDA escorts them to the door, where she stops them)*

FREDA Er, one question before you go. That money – in his back pocket. A fiver you said?

FRANK Aye, a crisp fiver, sometimes more. You didn't know? Sorry about that Freda.

ELI I reckon Seth could be buying St. Peter a hot toddy as we speak.

FRANK More like putting it on the slate....

BLACKOUT.

MUSIC.

End of Scene 2.

ALL BALLS AND ASHES

ACT 1.

Scene 3.

The Cloggers Arms. Set as for Scene 1. GEORGE is behind the bar, polishing glasses. FRANK and ELI enter.

ELI — You were dead right, George. By heck, Freda is a hard woman if I ever saw one.

GEORGE — No joy then?

FRANK — No, and no flipping ashes.

ELI — I reckon she wouldn't give you the snot off the end of her nose.

FRANK — There's no accounting for women. When Seth was at home and it came to housework, Freda couldn't abide him under her feet. Used to turn him out – once he'd done the housework.

ELI — Now he's turned to ash she wants to mother him. Got him so's she can keep her beady eye on him morning, noon and night, whilst at night time, the poor lad has to watch her slipping in and out of her nightie. Can you imagine a fate worse than that?

(FRANK and ELI go and sit at the table.)

GEORGE — Oh, I don't know. *(Thinks about it and then shudders)* No, maybe you're right. Makes a change though, Seth once told me as how she used to lock him out of the bedroom most nights in case he got ideas.

FRANK And now he's harmless she wants to lock him in...

ELI It's not right keeping a man away from the comfort of his hot water bottle. Not natural. Besides, he had cold feet did Seth. Needed his hottie.

GEORGE He told you that?

ELI No, it was her at number 9, Annie Pogson. She'd had a few like women do and let it slip. Said it was one thing she held against Seth.

FRANK By the sound of things, it wasn't the only thing she held against Seth. I mean, how would she know, unless...

(They exchange knowing looks. GEORGE approaches with two pints.)

ELI No Mary tonight, George?

GEORGE Took the news about Seth badly. Never seen a woman so upset. She's nipped out for a bit of fresh air. She'll be back shortly, meanwhile, here am I rushed off my feet. Don't know whether I'm coming or going...

FRANK *(looking round empty bar.)* Really? I don't know how on earth you manage, George.

GEORGE That Freda business. You should have sent someone with more tact – someone who has – you know – a way with women...

FRANK And you have? I don't know how you manage to hide all your talents.

ELI Ere, did you know that woman has Seth locked away in her bedroom?

GEORGE — *(astonished)* Gerraway! I thought he'd been cremated! Are you saying she's got him in her bedroom – stuffed? Isn't there a law against that?

ELI — Don't be daft! He's been cremated all right, Freda showed us the urn. Right fancy, it is. Keeps it on the sideboard, then come night time, she takes it up to the bedroom..

FRANK — 'Ere, George. Did you know he went to the crem in his cricketing clobber?

GEORGE — Really? That was nice of the old codger. Thinking of the lads and the game to the end, eh?

ELI — That was what we thought, until Freda told us it was her choice. Wanted to get shut of them...

FRANK — I've just had another thought; about what Freda said about Seth and cricket practice. Except getting together around this table and talking about it, we haven't had any practice...

GEORGE — Only practice you've had is lifting pints.

ELI — Then, if he wasn't practising, where was he?

FRANK — He loved bird–watching.

ELI — Bird–watching – at night?

GEORGE — And why not. There's bats, owls and them night jar things...

FRANK — Oh, he's got a night jar all right. A fancy urn all to himself. Mind you, it could have been worse.

ELI — How worse?

FRANK — She might have put him under the bed, amongst the fluff and next to the chamber pot.

GEORGE How would you know she's got a chamber pot?

FRANK I live next door, remember. Some houses still have outside privies and they've got chamber pots. I see them in the morning trotting down the garden with them.

ELI And she had Seth nipping down the garden with it, come rain or shine.

FRANK That's right. There'd be a cup of tea in bed for her, then he'd be sent rushing down the garden with the old pot. By heck. I can picture him now jogging along the path, nightshirt flapping in the breeze.

ELI Poor beggar. What sort of life as he got now? Forced to stare all night at 'er all covered in cold cream, hair in curlers, flannelette nightie, false teeth in a glass and a fag first thing in the morning. He must be turning in his grave.

FRANK He'll have a job seeing as he was cremated.

GEORGE At least there's one blessing.

FRANK And what is that?

GEORGE He won't have to empty the chamber pot.

(Enter MARY – unseen by others. She busies herself behind the bar.)

ELI Now talking of ashes. What are we going to do? There's no chance of keeping our promise unless frosty face Freda has a change of heart. Which one of us is brave enough to knock on her door and force her to hand them over.

(MARY is suddenly interested.)

GEORGE I'd rather face an angry bull.

FRANK Or cow.

GEORGE Can't see there's much difference.

FRANK I suppose we could always try something else.

ELI Alright, super brain, what?

FRANK Well, what about – nicking em?

GEORGE You mean – steal? I don't want no criminals in this pub. Got my reputation to think of. And I thought you were the brains of this outfit. Just think about it, for starters you'd never get past the door. If you did it would be like committing suicide.

ELI George is right, if you got past the chain and the locks you'd be doomed. Any more bright ideas?

(They think – FRANK finally, has something.)

FRANK As matter of fact, I believe I have. I reckon we will have no trouble getting in, that'll be easy. It's the getting out that might be the problem.

ELI We?

FRANK Yes, we. We can go in the same way as Seth. All those houses have old coal chutes. Now if he was late back from the Cloggers or his bird–watching and Freda had locked him out, Seth used to climb in through the chute and doss down on the settee. I've done it myself.

GEORGE You mean you climbed into Seth's house? You brave beggar...

FRANK No, you daft pillock. Into my own house.

ELI Frank is right. Eli used to brag about how he got in. She knew about it but thought it was his penance.

GEORGE The things chaps have to put up with women. I reckon

inventing lasses was God's big mistake. Should have stuck to men, snakes and apples. The world would have been a much safer place.

(Unseen behind the bar MARY reacts – silently.)

ELI — You might be right, George, but it's a bit late for him to change his mind. Now Frank, this coal–hole, you reckon one of us could get in – and steal the ashes…

GEORGE — Hang on, lads. This sounds like burglary – not so sure I like this stealing bit.

ELI — Alright, then. How about – purloin. That suit you?

GEORGE — *(thinks)* Aye. I reckon it'll do.

ELI — So, we – purloin the ashes – right from under her nose?

GEORGE — Ah, but what happens when she wakes up and finds them – purloined? She has built–in radar, she'll know who took them. I wouldn't want to be around then.

FRANK — I say it needs thinking about.

(FRANK sinks deep into his thinking mode, which involves scrunching himself up, eyes closed, with the fingers of both hand splayed across his forehead. GEORGE is concerned.)

GEORGE — Is he – is he alright?

ELI — Oh, aye. Frank has these moments, until all of a sudden he has a sort of cranial combustion and his whole brain lights up with a bright idea. He once came up with a great idea to stop the Titanic from sinking.

GEORGE — Don't you think it's a bit late for that?

ELI — You don't let little things like that get in the way of – thinking. And I didn't say his ideas always work.

GEORGE That's right, fill me with confidence.

(FRANK comes bolt upright)

FRANK *(excitedly)* Ah yes, I do believe I've got it!

ELI There you are, George. Told you so – cranial combustion, never fails. *(To FRANK)* So, what is it, super brain?

(All three move closer together, conspiratorially.)

FRANK *(emphasising every word)* The answer is – unless – she – doesn't – know...

ELI *(disappointed)* I thought you were the clever one. Of course Freda will know. She'll have Interflora out before she's got her teeth in and her slippers on.

GEORGE Interpol, you pillock. Sounds like another Titanic idea, if you ask me. It would be mission impossible. Like taking a pint from under Eli's nose. He'd know straight away something was not right.

FRANK Ah, but here's the clever bit. Would Eli notice if the pint was replaced by another?

ELI I would if I was paying for it. But tell me, would I get to keep the first one?

GEORGE Not if I have my way. Got my profits to think about...

ELI; This replacement. I reckon you have some explaining to do, Frank.

FRANK It's simple. The ashes are in an urn, right? So, we take the ashes and leave the urn.

ELI Wouldn't work. I'll wager she checks them night and day to make sure none of his bits have gone missing. Better think of something else, Einstein.

GEORGE	But would she know if the ash was replaced with something else, like... like...
FRANK	That's it, George. You're almost a genius. Hit the nail on the head. We replace 'em with fire grate ash.
GEORGE	By gum, lads! Brilliant! Between the pair of you you're not as dumb as you look... Now all we've got to do is to make sure we keep it secret – just between the three of us – right?
ELI;`	Right, we know what with and how – but when?
FRANK	What about tomorrow night. There'll be a full moon, lads...
GEORGE	What say we all meet at position A after I've done here.
ELI	That'll give us time to organise the band and the Morris men.
	(MARY quietly slips out and returns – she coughs and pretends to take her coat off – GEORGE sees.)
FRANK	Ah, Mary. Feeling better?
MARY	Oh, much. And I've had a very intriguing few minutes.
GEORGE	Good, then you're just in time – One of these lads has just had a brilliant idea. *(Pause for effect)* He's buying a round!

BLACKOUT.

MUSIC.

End of Scene 3.

ALL BALLS AND ASHES

ACT 1.

Scene 4.

The Cloggers Arms again. Empty stage. MARY enters with a bucket and a mop. She starts cleaning the floor, humming to herself. There's a knock at the door and then rattling as though the door is being shaken.

MARY *(calling)* You're too late – we're closed!

(More urgent knocking)

MARY *(calling)* Did you not hear? It's gone eleven o'clock. Pub's closed!

VERA *(offstage)* That you Mary Bushall? It's Vera – Vera Bottomley – is George there?

(MARY exits. We hear bolts being drawn.)

MARY *(offstage in surprise)* Vera Bottomley? And – Dolly!

DOLLY *(sweeping in, followed by VERA and MARY)* Mrs Cruickshanks to you.

MARY Yes, well, er – ladies – what on earth are you doing here at this time of night? I hardly think you're on a pub–crawl. Last time I saw you in here was five or six years ago…

DOLLY Seven years, three months…

VERA …and four days to be precise.

DOLLY Only then because it was being used as…

VERA …a polling station. A pub crawl, indeed! We've got better things…

DOLLY ...to do with our time.

MARY Like what?

VERA A word with...

DOLLY ...the so–called landlord George, for starters.

MARY George! What about?

DOLLY Our husbands.

MARY Husbands? What have they been up to?

VERA Thought George could...

DOLLY ... tell us.

VERA That maybe his beer's...

DOLLY ... been affecting them.

MARY Well, George isn't here at the moment. You've just missed him – said he had some business to attend to. Left me to clear up. But maybe I can help?

VERA You might. It's Frank, see. He's been acting strange all day...

MARY Stranger than usual, you mean?

DOLLY Eli too, like pacing the room...

VERA ...all nervous and shifty.

DOLLY ... Jumped like mad when I spoke. When I asked him if owt was wrong – he snapped my head off. Not like my Eli. He hasn't snapped at me in ten years or more. Not that he dare mind you.

VERA My Frank has been just the same, only worse. Nowty as a constipated greyhound.

DOLLY Mine starts rummaging . I asked what he was looking for he said something about his old army uniform. I was beginning to think we were at war.

MARY But they should be home by now – surely? They left just before George.

VERA ...That's it. They're not – at home that is...

DOLLY ...I'll give Eli his due – he might spend time here...

VERA ...but never stops out...

DOLLY ...late. Regular as...

VERA ... clockwork... Normally, they come home...

DOLLY ... flop into bed...

VERA ... and that's the last we hear of them...

DOLLY ... until the morning...

VERA I came across Dolly – looking...

DOLLY ...worried what we might...

VERA ...find. I mean, you...

DOLLY ...hear all sorts, 'specially when...

VERA ...there's a full moon...

DOLLY ...and bellies are full of...

VERA ...beer...

DOLLY ... especially beer. That's why we came...

VERA ...looking.

DOLLY ...don't normally frequent public...

VERA ... houses, but...

MARY *(cutting in)* But in this instance, you thought you would be brave and make an exception. Well, I'm sorry, Frank and Eli aren't here. Neither is George, he left me to tidy up. But then, now you mention it, both Frank and Eli were behaving suspiciously all evening. George too. Because they're always acting a bit strange, I didn't think of it at the time, but... *(Suddenly realising something)* Er, did you say there's a full moon? Strange – that was what Frank said – amongst other things. Then there was position A, whatever that is. Ladies, I think we ought to sit down and have a chat about this. *(She points to the table and chairs.)*

VERA What – you mean...

DOLLY ... sit down ...here? This table has been cleaned – hasn't it?

MARY Of course, did it myself.

(VERA and DOLLY reluctantly sit.)

DOLLY So what is there...

VERA ... to talk about?

MARY Something I overheard last night.

VERA Go on...

MARY Didn't catch all of it, only that it concerned Freda and Seth's ashes, there was talk about a brass band and Morris men. Oh, and pinching beer from under Eli's nose.

DOLLY Bet that didn't go down well.

VERA What'll they want with a brass band?

DOLLY That'll be the beer talking.

MARY Frank also said something about fire grate ash and there being a full moon tonight and they would meet at position A.

VERA Definitely the beer. And what then?

MARY Isn't that enough? I only know they had their heads together and I knew they were up to something.

DOLLY So, what do...

VERA ... we do?

MARY We? Now ladies, they are your husbands. Grown up – sensible men – well, some of the time – and if they can't look after themselves, it's a poor look out. I suggest you go home and they'll turn up. Probably waiting for you even as we speak.

DOLLY That the best...

VERA ...advice you can give? I mean...

DOLLY ...when the husbands of two respectable ladies...

VERA ... go missing – well...

MARY What do you expect me to do – call missing persons? You go home ladies, I'll shortly be taking a walk myself and I'll keep an eye open. I'm sure they'll be fine....

DOLLY Well, if you...

VERA ...say so.

BLACKOUT.

MUSIC.

End of Scene 4.

ALL BALLS AND ASHES

ACT 1.

Scene 5

Night, outside FREDA's house. There is a coal chute in front of the wall and a sash window high up on the wall. (SEE SET PLANS) We hear an owl hoot and then a cat miaowing. FRANK and ELI enter. They are wearing balaclavas and they have their faces blackened, SAS style. They are carrying torches. GEORGE follows with a carrier bag. ELI is carrying a steel army helmet and he stops and puts it on. They all speak in loud whispers.

GEORGE What the hell do you want that for?

ELI Took me ages to find it and I'm not taking any chances. You mark my words, this could be a war–zone.

GEORGE War zone? Don't be daft.

(From the open bedroom window above comes the sound of snoring.)

FRANK Hear that, Eli? Does that sound like a war zone?

ELI Does to me. She could be bluffing, waiting with something deadly. Who knows what she might chuck out of her window.

GEORGE Like what – her duvet?

ELI There's that chamber pot for starters.

(More snoring)

FRANK Don't know about any war or chamber pots, but how the hell can a man have his final rest with that racket going on every night? *(He carefully removes the coal chute cover)*

FRANK There you are, lads. The cover's off, the first part of operation – deception.

(They peer into a black hole.)

ELI Doesn't look very inviting.

FRANK It does if you're a bag of nutty slack.

GEORGE Look at it this way. Beyond that hole there could be the stairway to Heaven.

ELI Gateway to hell, more likely.

GEORGE Like Frank said – it'll be dead easy.

ELI Dead? Must you use that word?

GEORGE Sorry. So who's going in for a re–union with Seth?

(There is no answer.)

GEORGE Well, don't all speak at once. Maybe you'd like to hold a committee meeting.

ELI Speaking personally, I know if I went in and she saw me – she'd kill me.

FRANK And I am allergic to death. What about you George?

GEORGE She'd murder me if I was caught in her bedroom and then who'd look after the pub?

FRANK Do you think we ought to call it off?

GEORGE Courage, mes enfants. Remember the Alamo.

(ELI and FRANK give GEORGE strange looks.)

GEORGE Don't you give me funny looks, just because I speak a bit of foreign.

ELI If you're dishing out the courage talks, why don't you climb in and get the ash?

GEORGE Oh, no. I only came along to see fair play, besides you're the one wearing camouflage.

FRANK Looks like it's between you and me, Eli. We'll toss for it. *(Produces coin)* Call, Eli.

ELI Right. Heads I win. Tails you lose.

(The coin is tossed – FRANK doesn't know why he has lost. Grumbling he disappears into the coal chute – then quickly re–appears.)

FRANK But what if she sees me?

GEORGE I thought that had been settled. She'll kill you.

FRANK How do I get round that?

ELI Simple. Don't resist. That way it'll be quick and painless.

GEORGE On the other hand you could make out you're the ghost of Seth's past, come to have your wicked way with her. That'll either shut her up or put a smile on her face. Now will you get on with it, we haven't got all night.

(FRANK once more disappears into the chute.)

GEORGE Bloody amateurs! Don't know why I put up with you.

ELI Because we keep you in business, that's why.

(FRANK re–appears.)

ELI I see you're still in the land of the living. What is it this time? A change of underwear, or you feel the sudden urge to write out your will?

FRANK I've forgotten the ash. Who's got it?

(GEORGE holds out the carrier bag. From it he produces a large tin of coffee.)

FRANK A coffee tin? Couldn't you have found something more dignified than that?

GEORGE Best I could do at short notice. Mind you, it's best coffee. Two for the price of one – none of your cheap stuff.

FRANK And the ash?

GEORGE Like we agreed; it came from the log fire in the snug.

ELI I'm sure Seth would appreciate the thought. Now can we get on with it?

(With the help of ELI – FRANK disappears – then returns.)

Hell's bells, Frank, you're like a bloody yoyo, What is it this time?

(FRANK snatches off ELI'S tin hat and jams it on his own head.)

Here! What did you do that for?

FRANK Like you said, this could be a war–zone and if I'm going to go, I want some protection.

(FRANK disappears. Others feign nonchalance but are frightened by the hoot of an owl.)

GEORGE What was that?

ELI I'm not sure but I have a bad feeling about this. I don't think I should be here.

FREDA *(from offstage (top window)* Is – is there anyone there?

ELI Hey oop! You hear that. That was Freda. Sounds like our man has made contact...

(More silence – broken by the loud ringing sound offstage of the chamber pot being hit by the steel helmet.)

FREDA *(offstage)* Is there – anyone there? Is – is that – you, Seth? *(There is a second clang of metal against a chamber pot. Light comes on in FREDA'S bedroom. A loud, blood curdling scream, thuds – more silence – the light goes out)*

GEORGE Oh, my Lord! He's done for! She's killed him! I knew it would go wrong!

(As ELI dithers there is a rhythmic squeaking sound and glow of a torch from offstage.)

ELI There's someone coming. She's called for re–enforcements. It's a pincer movement, we'll be caught like rats in a trap. I'm off... *(ELI exits stage right.)*

GEORGE *(unaware ELI has left)* Here, I know that sound. It's Dawson, the local bobby. Don't worry, Eli, I know how to deal with him. Eli? Eli?

(DAWSON the local police sergeant enters, pushing an ancient, squeaking bicycle and flashing his torch.)

DAWSON Hello, hello. What have we here then?

GEORGE Er – evening Sergeant. It's me, George, from the Cobblers. Just – just...

(GEORGE blusters. Behind DAWSON, FRANK pops his head out of the coal hole. He is minus the tin hat.)

FRANK Here! Will someone tell me what's going on?

(DAWSON jumps – turns and sees FRANK.)

DAWSON By the chief constable's truncheon, you fair made me jump, young fellow. Nearly had me out of my boots. And who the hell are you and what are you doing down there? *(Shines his torch into FRANK's face and peers closely.)*

DAWSON 'Ere, I know you don't I? Frank Bottomley, isn't it?

(FRANK vigorously shakes his head in denial.)

GEORGE Ah, that's right, Sergeant, Frank Bottomley. Very observant of you.

DAWSON Oh, we're highly trained observers, you know. Can tell a crime a mile off. Nothing gets past the boys in blue. And what has Bottomley got to say for himself?

FRANK Er evening, officer.

DAWSON Well, that will do for starters. Now I know it may sound a silly question, George, but maybe you can explain what Bottomley is doing half in – half out of a coal hole?

GEORGE Yes, that is a silly – no, I mean a very good question, Sarge. It's like this...*(GEORGE thinks.)*

DAWSON I'm waiting, George. And it had better be good.

GEORGE Oh, it is. Fact is, it's so good you won't believe it. Er, the silly sod had a little too much to drink in the Cloggers. He's not quite himself – you know how when some begin to lose their faculties, they can get quite stupid after a pint or two.

DAWSON That is very true.

GEORGE Didn't want any trouble – so I thought I would see him home – for safety's sake.

(FRANK has cottoned on, puts on a silly, drunken grin as DAWSON shines his torch on him.)

DAWSON Stupid, you say? Aye, you're right there. It‘s clear he‘s all of that. Here, he wasn‘t driving was he?

GEORGE What, all of fifty yards, Sarge!? Besides, he hasn't got a car...

DAWSON Now that's a pity. But on the other hand this is what I like to see. A landlord thinking of his customers, his community and the law. *(He takes a closer look at FRANK's blackened face)*

DAWSON By the heck, lad. I'll say this. You could do with a good wash.

GEORGE That's what you get for using the coal chute, Sarge.

DAWSON I'm not a complete fool, I can work that one out. But what I don't understand is what is this poor creature doing in a coal–hole?

GEORGE By gum, you ask some good questions, Sarge. You see – the daft beggar forgot his key. Was locked out, so – I thought I'd take charge. Wouldn't do to disturb Vera, the little lady, now, would it? I'm sure you know what it's like, one tiny innocent slip and they nag you about it for weeks after...

DAWSON Oh, I do indeed. I do indeed. Well, I'll leave you to it, lads.

(He turns to leave, but then shines his torch first on FREDA'S door, number 17. Then next door.)

DAWSON 'Ello, 'ello. I believe I see what you're up to. I've sussed you out. Like I said, we're not a trained observers for nothing...

GEORGE You've sussed us out? Oh, Lord, er what do you mean, Sarge?

DAWSON Yes. I see it all now. Fact is on the evidence before me I should take you in to custody...

FRANK But – but what for, Sarge?

DAWSON At the very least, stupidity...*(He produces his notebook and licks a pencil.)*

GEORGE Custody? Stupidity? Hang about, Sarge. It was all his idea – I'm only...

DAWSON *(cutting in)* Passing the buck, are we? Now that is a sure sign of guilt. Won't do you any good, you've already admitted it and we can both see he's incapable..

GEORGE Admitted what?

DAWSON Earlier you said. you were in charge. Now I'll start with a simple question, George. Are you sober?

GEORGE As a judge, Sarge.

DAWSON That's no recommendation for a start. Second question Are you sane?

GEORGE Sane as you, Sarge. But why the questions?

DAWSON Reason I ask , is because this chap is Frank Bottomley, but you're delivering him to the wrong house. This is number 17 and as I recall this chap lives next door at number 18...

GEORGE By heck you're right, Sarge. I'll say this for you, you're a smart one.

DAWSON Very true. But I can see how easy it is to make a mistake with all these houses looking the same and gormless here in no fit state. Tell you what, I'll give you a hand, can't have him disturbing the wrong woman now can we? Even worse, we might wake her husband and he could easily get the wrong idea. Then where would we be?

GEORGE In the land of bloody miracles, Sarge.

(The 'drunken' FRANK is hauled out of the coal hole and escorted offstage. DAWSON returns brushing himself down and collects his bicycle.)

DAWSON Good job one of us was awake, George. Job done, nothing to report, that's the way I like it. Another quiet night. The citizens of Greenbridge can sleep safely in their beds tonight.

GEORGE Just as you say, Sarge. A quiet night. All safe and sound.

DAWSON Now George, having secured the nation. Do you think there might be something suspicious round the back of the Cloggers around two o'clock that you would like investigating? I believe I might be in the mood for making a report about then?

GEORGE But of course, Sarge. Would that be one pint or two?

DAWSON Oh, I think getting Bottomley safely home is worth two pints, don't you?

(DAWSON cycles off. FRANK returns and ELI re–appears.)

FRANK By heck. I thought he'd rumbled us..

GEORGE You played being stupid to perfection, Frank. Guess you must have been practising. Couldn't have done better myself.

ELI Did you get the ash, lad?

FRANK Of course. Just managed to hide it when I saw Dawson.

(FRANK retrieves the coffee tin now containing Seth's ashes. MARY appears, lurking in the shadows.)

ELI We thought Freda had done for you.

FRANK I was lucky to get out alive. Talk about being in the lion's den.

GEORGE Go on, give us all the sexy bits.

FRANK First off, I was right about that chamber pot. I was crawling round her bed and went slap into it. Didn't half make a sound, it was like clobbering the church clock...

GEORGE Aye, we heard. Then what?

FRANK It woke her up, so – I did the sensible thing...

ELI That would be a first.

FRANK I remembered my army training. Kept my head down until it went quiet. Then off again like a tiger stalking its prey. Then I went straight into another chamber pot. That woman has got the whole bedroom booby–trapped with them. If that wasn't enough, the bloody tin hat fell off. Dropped straight onto the second chamber pot. Sounded just like Big Ben and that woke her up good and proper.

GEORGE And what happened next?

FRANK I played it cool. Lay there until I thought she'd dropped off and then popped my head up. But she hadn't – dropped off I mean. On came the light and there she was, all curlers, no teeth and pink frilly nightie. For a moment we were eyeball to eyeball, face cream to stubble.

ELI So what did you do?

FRANK Thought I'd be friendly like – so I smiled...

GEORGE You smiled?

FRANK Yes, I don't know who screamed louder – her or me. Then she passed out and that was my chance. Did the switch with Seth's ashes, turned the light out and legged it for the cellar. Next thing I know Dawson of the Mounties is here and I'm being hauled off and stuffed into my own coal chute. Mind you, it could have been worse.

GEORGE What's worse than being man–handled by Dawson?

FRANK All that commotion stuffing me in my own coal chute could have woken *my* wife, then there would have been hell to pay.

ELI Here, you don't think Dawson suspected anything, do you?

GEORGE Only that Frank was pissed as a newt and I was stuffing him arse first into the wrong coal chute. But I don't think he'll suspect anything as long as he gets his two pints in the early hours.

GEORGE We might have the ash, lads. But I'm a bit worried about the rest of it. I mean, I hope you've organised the Morris men and brass band, lads.

FRANK Er, well, yes. Don't worry, it's all arranged.

(MARY decides to make herself visible, pretending to be out walking.)

MARY Arranged! What's all arranged?

(The three men jump.)

ELI Bloody hell, Mary! What the devil are you doing out this time of night? Thought you were poorly...

MARY I like walking at this time of night. But I asked the question first. What are you doing out this late?

FRANK Just paying our respects to Seth, Mary.

MARY What! At midnight? Does Freda know?

ELI She probably does by now.

GEORGE So, are you feeling better, lass?

MARY The fresh air's done me a power of good...

GEORGE Well, you get off now and get your beauty sleep, lass. See you tomorrow, eh?

(MARY is reluctant to leave.)

MARY You seem anxious to get rid of me? Well, all right then. Good night...Oh, before I go, Vera and Dolly were out looking for you.

FRANK and ELI — They were!? And?

MARY — Told them to go home – that you knew what you were doing. Now I'm not so sure... *(MARY exits)*

GEORGE — That was close, lads. Not once but twice.

ELI — Just as well she didn't see the tin hat. Then she really would have been suspicious. Here, Frank, what have you done with it?

FRANK — Like I say, it dropped off. Oh, bloody hell, the tin hat! Sorry, Eli, but it's still there, under Freda's bed.

ELI — And it can stay there. I'm not risking the wrath of Hades. *(Thinks)* Oh, Lord. I hope she can't find her reading glasses.

GEORGE — Why's that, Eli?

ELI — Because, George. It's got my name, rank and number on it, that's why!

BLACKOUT.

MUSIC.

End of ACT 1.

HOUSE LIGHTS.

INTERVAL.

ALL BALLS AND ASHES

ACT 11.

Scene 1.

The cricket field – Jasper's Bottom – later that night. There is a bench (or two chairs), a cricket scoreboard (could be on the side of a "shed") and some shrubbery. An owl is hooting. The set is empty until the VICAR enters, carrying a telescope (for stargazing). He takes a swig from his hip flask, then, hearing someone approaching, he ducks down behind some shrubbery at the rear of the stage, where he is visible to the audience but not to FRANK, ELI and GEORGE who now enter. FRANK is carrying the coffee tin, containing Seth's ashes and a large carrier bag. He places the carrier bag at the side of the stage.

GEORGE Right, we're here. Never been to a scattering before. So, what's next?

ELI We start the ceremony, I guess.

GEORGE Ceremony? That sounds a bit religious. We'll only be short of the vicar.

ELI Vicar? Being as what we are about is not quite with the consent of the next of kin, it's hardly surprising the vicar wasn't invited. Apart from Freda, he's the last one I'd like to see here.

FRANK You know, I reckon we were Seth's next of kin, being as it seems we saw more of him than did Freda. So we'd best get on with it. Do we all know what we're doing?

ELI I'm looking after the brass band.

FRANK I'm seeing to the Morris men.

GEORGE What Morris Men and what band? I don't see them.

FRANK Don't worry George. It's all taken care of. So, what are you going to do?

GEORGE Me? I'm here out of respect for Seth. Seems I've got the best job. Nowt to do but sit back and enjoy it all.

FRANK I have a feeling that's where you are wrong, George.

ELI I'm off to sort the band out. Give me a shout when you're ready. *(ELI exits)*

GEORGE I have to say I was beginning to doubt you. The Morris men, the brass band? It's all a matter of trust, eh?

FRANK That's right, George. So, the ceremony begins.

GEORGE Can't bloody wait. The suspense is killing me.

(FRANK proceeds to roll up his trouser legs. From the carrier bag he produces bells which he ties around his legs. Next a flowered hat, then traditional sticks and a tape recorder which he switches on. Out of it comes a traditional Morris dance. GEORGE watches open–mouthed as FRANK starts the Morris Dance.)

FRANK Morris men couldn't come, George. Had to borrow this lot. So come on, roll up your trouser legs, get those bells on, put a fancy hat on and get stuck in.

(A bemused GEORGE reluctantly obeys.)

GEORGE So – is this it?

FRANK 'Fraid so, George. All the Morris men were otherwise engaged.

What did you expect, the Huddersfield choral society? It's all up to us, George to uphold the integrity of the Greenbridge Players. I only hope Seth appreciates it. Mind you when the band gets here we'll have some proper music.

GEORGE Eli has got a band then? It's not just the two of us playing a drum, a cymbal and a triangle. If it is I'd best warn you, I can't play a note.

FRANK Oh, there's a brass band, the very best in fact. Eli managed to get Black Dyke – he's sorting them out right now...

GEORGE *(stops dead in his tracks)* Black Dyke? Eee, lad, that must have taken some doing. I take my hat off to the pair of you. You've fair done Eli proud.

FRANK I have to admit it took quite a bit of – negotiation. I'll just see if they're ready. *(To ELI – off–stage)* Band ready, Eli?

ELI *(offstage)* Almost. Just need sorting...

GEORGE *(still dancing but already beginning to get out of breath)* This is all a bit – weird. I mean – there's Black Dyke waiting in the wings. *(Pant)* You and me – dressed like Morris Men. *(Pant)* Suppose someone sees us?

FRANK *(stops dancing)* Don't be daft, George. What stupid pillock *(Pant)* would be about at this time of night?

(VICAR raises his head above the shrubbery. FRANK resumes dancing.)

GEORGE And then there's *(Pant)* Seth's ashes. That's even weirder.

FRANK Ah, yes. Well, think of it like this. *(Pant)* It's best quality bone meal – good for the grass *(Pant)* and the wicket.

GEORGE True. Er, do you think *(Pant)* we ought to say a prayer? *(Pant)* I mean, it's like putting him in the ground...

FRANK — By heck, that's a good idea, George. *(To ELI – offstage)* Eli! Can you hold the band back for a few seconds? *(Pant)* We're saying a prayer for Seth.

ELI — *(offstage)* Good idea. I'll come and join you.

(ELI enters. FRANK switches off Morris music, puts his hands together and noisily clears his throat. GEORGE and ELI do likewise.)

FRANK — For what the cricket ground is about to receive – may we all be truly thankful, especially Seth. Amen.

GEORGE — Amen.

ELI — Amen.

VICAR — AaaaMen.

(The trio hear the last amen and exchange puzzled looks. ELI exits.)

ELI — *(offstage)* Band's all ready to go, Frank!

FRANK — Right! Now I don't know whether this is what you had in mind, Seth, but I reckon this is the best we can do. Right Eli. Bring on the band!

(Impressive sound of brass off–stage. From his hiding place an astonished VICAR looks on. ELI enters stage left pushing a pram with a tape recorder in it belting out. He starts to do a circuit of the stage. FRANK and GEORGE are still performing a Morris dance with FRANK scattering Seth's ashes. The VICAR steps out, seen by FRANK who comes to an abrupt halt. GEORGE and ELI are oblivious and continue.)

VICAR — *(shouting)*What – what on earth is going on?

(ELI – carried away by the brass band – has made a temporary exit. GEORGE comes face to face with the VICAR, but continues to dance.)

GEORGE Oh, Lord!

FRANK Not quite, but you're not far out, George.

VICAR Would someone please tell me what is going on?

GEORGE *(still dancing.)* We – we...

VICAR It would help if you would stand still for a moment.

(GEORGE – almost on his knees – stops dancing.)

GEORGE Thank God for that! *(Pant)* I've run out of breath!

VICAR Now did I hear a brass band? Where is it?

(As he speaks ELI returns. Circles the stage – then runs into the VICAR.)

ELI Oh, my God!

FRANK We've done that bit, Eli. It's the Vicar, you know – the one you said wasn't coming?

VICAR What on earth is going on?

GEORGE Well, it's not a Vicar's tea–party.

VICAR I've worked that one out. But what on earth is that in the pram?

ELI Ah, if you think it's a baby, then you're wrong., Vicar. That is Black Dyke Brass band no less. *(VICAR steps forward, inspects the tape deck and switches it off.)* Well – it was.

VICAR And who the dickens are you?

ELI Hell's bells, Vicar. It's a fine state of affairs when the shepherd can't recognise one of his own flock. It's me, Vicar.

	Eli Cruickshanks!
VICAR	Eli? Good grief. Didn't recognise you with all that muck on your face.
ELI	This is not muck, Vicar. I'll have you know it is genuine, expensive camouflage from an army surplus store. Must be good, it fooled you.
VICAR	In this peaceful land, at this time in the morning do you really think there is a need for camouflage? Will someone please tell me what is going on?
	(FRANK is trying to conceal the coffee tin, but the VICAR has seen.)
FRANK	You see Vicar. It's – it's a little get together, you understand?
VICAR	I'm sorry, but I don't understand. And what is that thing you are hiding behind your back like a Sunday collecting box?
GEORGE	It's – it's – Seth's...
FRANK	*(elbowing GEORGE and cutting in)* Shut up, George. You're out of breath, remember?
VICAR	Well, gentlemen I'm waiting for an explanation.
FRANK	I can explain everything, Vicar. In this tin we have a – mixture of – of...
GEORGE	Herbs and spice....
FRANK	Er, yes. Herbs and spice – oh, and a touch of – bone meal...
VICAR	Bone meal – but what for
GEORGE	To sprinkle over the wicket. It's an ancient, local custom...
ELI	*(catching on)* That's right. A sort of – fertility rite, goes back many years. A blessing of the cricket field that's

guaranteed to bring lots of runs to the home side and death and destruction to that other lot.

VICAR Fertility rite, eh? Sounds rather pagan to me. Can't say I altogether approve.

FRANK I suppose some would call it – a fertility ceremony in reverse.

VICAR And a brass band and Morris men. But why this hour in the morning?

GEORGE Think about it, Vicar, it's the only time we can all get together. I mean, take me, I run the pub and this lot's usually in it.

VICAR It all seems so very strange to me.

ELI Ah, but so's wandering around at this time of night with a telescope. I mean – if someone – normally so respected – was by chance seen wandering about the village in the early hours. Well, you never know what people might think.

VICAR Oh, I assure you it's perfectly innocent. I've been observing Venus. I've had my eye on her for some time.

(GEORGE gives him a nudge with his elbow.)

GEORGE Oh, aye. Didn't know you were the sort, Vicar.

ELI Isn't that her at number…?

VICAR I mean Venus, the planet in the sky.

GEORGE, ELI and FRANK *(in unison)* Of course, that one. *(They all point to the sky – but each in a different direction.)*

VICAR Now, did I hear you mention our dearly departed Seth Hegginbotham?

FRANK Did we? Oh, yes. This is a little something to help our old pal on his way. He loved Morris men and brass bands. Loved everybody, even the church. Was very appreciative of you, Vicar.

VICAR Really? Well, I admit I did have a soft spot for Seth. Just wish he'd shown his appreciation by attending church more often. However, by way of returning the compliment, do you think I could – join in? I've always fancied a little Morris dancing. *(VICAR is already rolling up his trouser legs, has taken a handkerchief and sticks from the carrier bag. Turns on the tape player and begins to dance. The others watch, then one by one join in. ELI is the last. With a shrug of his shoulders he throws himself into the dance. Unseen by those on stage, MARY appears in the background shrubbery. Meanwhile FRANK can't stop the VICAR helping himself from the coffee tin. VICAR sniffs at it.)*

VICAR Herbs and spices you say. Any particular variety?

FRANK Just about everything. Chives, Parsley, Thyme, a bit of ginger.

VICAR Oh, I like a bit of ginger. And we scatter it – anywhere?

ELI Anywhere you like, Vicar.

VICAR My, this is splendid. We must *(Pant)* do this more often. I'll make a note in the parish magazine under say – country pursuits?

(MARY exits. ELI also exits stage left, leaving the others still dancing on stage.)

VICAR A ceremony *(Pant)* to help *(Pant)* Seth on his way, did you say?

FRANK That's right, Vicar. A farewell *(Pant)* to a dearly loved departed chieftain.

(FRANK makes a run for it. VICAR is enjoying himself with exhausted GEORGE clinging to his coat tails.)

VICAR Oh, what fun. I am enjoying this.

GEORGE I'm glad someone is.

VICAR I could dance all night...

GEORGE I bloody hope not!

(GEORGE staggers offstage leaving the oblivious VICAR dancing by himself.)

BLACKOUT.

MUSIC grows louder.

End of Scene 1.

ALL BALLS AND ASHES

ACT 11.

Scene 2

The music continues until it grows fainter but still keeps playing. A spotlight appears, in which is a telephone table, with a telephone and telephone books. POTTS appears in the spotlight, doing up his dressing gown. His sleep has been disturbed and he is not happy.

POTTS	Damn and blast it! VANDALS! How dare they disturb my sleep! We'll soon put a stop to their little game... *(Picks up the telephone and dials)* 9 – 9 – *(He hesitates – thinks – at length)* Ah, yes. 9.
MARIGOLD	*(offstage)* Arnold, dear! What on earth is going on – and what is that noise?
POTTS	*(calling to her)* Sorry dear. Can't hear you for that damned racket going on outside. *(Pause)* Ah, operator? Oh, good. I was beginning to think I might get an answer phone. No, I'm not being rude. What service do I want? Oh, police, please – as quick as you can....
MARIGOLD	*(offstage)* Do come back to bed, dear. Is your back troubling you? I'll rub it for you if you wish.
POTTS	No need for that, Marigold dearest. I'm phoning the emergency services.

(MARIGOLD enters, also in a dressing gown.)

MARIGOLD The emergency services? Oh dear. Is your back that bad?

POTTS Hello? Hello! That the police? By George, you took your time. We could have been murdered in our beds. *(Pause)* No, I'm not George and I am not reporting a murder, yet... *(To Marigold)* Er, no, my back is fine, precious. *(Pause)* No, not you officer. You are not precious, I was speaking to my wife *(BEAT)* Who am I? Arnold Potts – for twenty years the highly regarded manager of the Greenbridge Bank and in that time, only one dissatisfied customer and I have a complaint. *(Pause)* No, my call has nothing to do with the dissatisfied customer. I want to report vandals, officer. *(Pause)* Yes, that is what I said. Van–dals. *(Pause)* What do you mean, have I got the registration number and what sort of van? Ah, a little joke, eh? Ha, ha, bloody ha. Yes, a very little joke...

(MARIGOLD is now rubbing his back.)

MARIGOLD Is that better dear?

POTTS Oh, yes, that is nice, my dear. You have the soothing touch of an angel. *(Pause)* Er, no, not you constable. Whatever it is – it's going off on the cricket field. *(Pause)* Hmm, nice, dearest. Perhaps – perhaps if you rub just a little lower down. *(Pause)* What's that officer? You want to know what is – lower down? *(Pause)* Oh, I assure you what is lower down has nothing to do with you. *(Pause)* No, officer, I am not withholding information. *(Pause)* Ah, that's the spot, my precious. *(Pause)* I am not speaking to you, officer, I am talking to my wife who is giving me a little rub. *(Pause)*

What is happening on the cricket field? Just one moment, if you'll kindly stay where you are, I shall go and have another look. *(Pause)* I have a large pair of Bi–noculars, you see. Yes, A very large pair – *(Pause)* What do you mean – you don't know what bi–noculars are and am I being indecent. *(Pause)* You've led a sheltered life? I see. *(Picks up the binoculars and trains them into the distance.)* Good Lord! Would you believe it! I think they are dancing and I can see – bare legs and someone dressed all in black. And there's that confounded band. *(Pause)* A brass band I do believe. *(Pause)* Oh, you quite like brass bands, do you? At one o'clock in the morning? Well, you are more than welcome to this one. *(Pause)* Do I know what they are playing? Of course not. What does it all mean, you ask? Well, you're the policeman. *(Pause)* I see, you'd like a few clues? Easy ones. Well, what about that person in black, and then the bare legs for starters. *(Pause)* Yes, bare legs – and dancing. No, at a guess I would say they are women. Probably one of those modern fertility rites, shouldn't wonder...

MARIGOLD Did you say dancing, Arnold? How lovely. Er, who are you talking to, dear?

POTTS Some precious policeman – I mean, a policeman, precious. *(Pause)* No, you are not precious officer. I am talking to Marigold and no, I haven't been drinking.

MARIGOLD You know dear, we haven't been dancing in years. I could put a record on if you wish. One of Victor Sylvester perhaps?

POTTS If you must dear, something by Victor sounds awfully nice. *(Pause)* What's that constable? You want to know who is Victor? Actually, my wife has a record... *(Pause)* No, no, not a police record. *(Pause)* The dancing? How would I know what sort of dancing – all I know is it's not a bloody barn dance.

MARIGOLD Arnold dear! Language! I won't let you dance with me if you use naughty words...

POTTS Sorry, precious. *(Pause)* Er, yes officer, I know it's an offence to swear at one of her majesty's constabulary. *(Pause)* You want to know what is happening? Well, at the moment my wife wants to dance to Victor Sylvester, whilst outside it appears those women are all dancing on Jasper's Bottom. *(Pause)* Yes, I did say Jasper's Bottom. *(Pause)* What is Jasper doing about it? Well, nothing; as far as I know the chap has been dead for some time. *(Pause)* No, I never met the fellow... *(Pause)* Now you are asking ridiculous questions. Vandals are disturbing my sleep and I want something done about it. *(Pause)* I beg your pardon – you would like to speak with my wife? Very well, then, be it at your peril. *(hands phone to MARIGOLD)* Don't know why, but the stupid policeman fellow wants to speak with you.

MARIGOLD Really? Oh, this is so exciting. Don't think I've spoken to a real policeman before. It's not Scotland Yard, is it? *(Takes telephone)* Er, yes, Mr Policeman...*(Pause)* Yes, that is absolutely correct, Mr Potts – Arnold that is – is my husband. And he is the manager of Greenbridge bank. Been the highly regarded manager of the bank for twenty years and in that time has only had one dissatisfied customer. *(Pause)* Oh, you know. Well, you could have said. *(Pause)* Er, no. he does not drink in moderation. *(Pause)* Yes, that's what I said. To be frank, I have no idea where this Moderation is. We do have a – Locomotion. Your Moderation doesn't sound a very reputable public house; it's probably full of young men on those scooter things. Very, very occasionally we do partake of a small drink in the Clogger's Arms, but only because it's local and we feel one should support local industry, shouldn't one? Use it or lose it, I believe they say. *(Pause)* Oh, yes. I am still talking about the local hostelry. And yes, Arnold is quite sound of mind – as I am sure you will have gathered. *(Pause)* What's that? You also like dancing – Oh *(Pause)*… only Latin! *(Pause)* Oh so do I – especially the Samba. Very nice. *(Pause)* You want to speak with my husband? Oh, do you have to? I was so enjoying our conversation. Well, if you must, please do not detain him, we're going to do a spot of dancing – to Victor Sylvester – you know. Isn't is exciting, never done it at such an early hour. I wonder what on earth the neighbours will think?

POTTS Marigold! Never mind what the neighbours might think. I demand that you give me that phone, immediately!

MARIGOLD There is no need to shout, Arnold, just because I find it exciting speaking to a policeman. *(MARIGOLD hands over the phone – and departs if a huff.)*

POTTS Now see here my man… *(Pause)* Oh, you prefer – Constable. Constable Harris. I see, well, are you going to do anything about these – these vandals? *(Pause)* You have a man on the ground and will pass the information to him? A Sergeant Dawson. Yes, I have heard of Dawson. And will this sergeant fellow act upon the information – tonight? *(Pause)* You – hope – so. What's that? It's hardly a matter for the flying squad and all depends on whether – his bicycle is working.? *(Looks through his binoculars again. It has suddenly gone quiet)* Well, it appears he might be too late, for it seems these vandals have left. Nevertheless, in the meantime Constable Harris, you may safely take it from me that my pen will be working overtime writing to your Chief Constable, as I intend telling him how you allowed these vandals to escape... Do you understand? *(Slams the telephone down and glares at it)* The man is a complete buffoon! A disgrace to the uniform!

MARIGOLD *(re–appears having cast off her dressing gown to reveal a diaphanous negligee. She speaks teasingly)* You shouted at me, you naughty boy! But I forgive you. Now are you ready, dear? To begin – would you prefer a slow romantic waltz – slow slinky foxtrot – or would you want to go the whole hog and indulge in – a very sexy tango? *(She melts into her husband's reluctant arms as the sound of the first bars of a Victor Sylvester dance number fill the stage.)*

BLACKOUT

End of Scene 2.

ALL BALLS AND ASHES

ACT 11.

Scene 3

The Cloggers Arms. Past midnight. GEORGE is behind the bar. There is a knock at the door. He goes offstage (we hear bolts being drawn) and returns followed by DAWSON.

DAWSON Sorry I'm a bit late, George. Haven't kept you up, have I?

GEORGE *(stifles a yawn)* Er, no, not at all Sarg. Funny hours are all the same to me.

DAWSON Well, it's certainly been a funny night. Started off nice and quiet, then there was you trying to stuff Bottomley in the wrong house. Good job I was on hand to put you right…

GEORGE One of life's little mistakes, Sarge. Could have happened to anyone. But there are compensations, like this. *(Produces a pint)* There, one suspicious package for you to investigate.

DAWSON *(tastes)* Hmm, seems all right to me. Now, where was I?

GEORGE A funny night…

DAWSON Ah, yes, more weird than funny. What with you and Bottomley, then a call from young Constable Harris down at the nick. He's new, wet behind the ears. Needs a bit of discipline and learning. Not like we were at his age. Anyway, he had me investigating an orgy.

GEORGE *(cutting in)* Did you say – orgy, as in – sex, Sarg? In Greenbridge? But where? I'd always hoped, I mean, didn't think they went in for that sort of thing here – more's the pity…

DAWSON Ah, not only sex, George, but also a suspicious death. Harris claimed he'd received a report someone by the name of Jasper had been trampled to death by a gang of women....

GEORGE Ooooh, nasty!

DAWSON That's what the caller told Harris. Sent me off to the cricket field to investigate...

GEORGE The cricket field? Surely not.

DAWSON I could have waited for back–up, but no, like a true defender of the public I went into the unknown to investigate...

GEORGE By yourself? Now that's what I call real bravery.

DAWSON If you say so, George. Truth is, I've never had one of them before, at least not all to myself. Had to share the last murder with half of the force.

(As DAWSON slurps GEORGE steps from behind the bar. One trouser leg is rolled up and he is still wearing bells around the leg.)

DAWSON That Arnold Potts fellow. You know him?

GEORGE The bank manager? Yes, he comes in occasionally.

DAWSON Has he – has he given you any trouble. Perhaps likes his drink – a little too much?

GEORGE With these business types it's hard to tell. Mind you, there have been occasions...

DAWSON *(cutting in)* Yes?

GEORGE When he's had a job getting his wallet out. Comes of being a bank manager, I suppose. So, what's he been up to?

DAWSON It was Potts who rang PC Wet Behind The Ears Harris. Claimed there was a brass band and naked women cavorted round the cricket field. Said they were dancing on a fellow called Jasper – that he was long dead...

GEORGE Naked women – cavorting on the cricket field? But there were no naked women. I mean – when?

DAWSON Exactly. By gum, you're sharp. Couldn't have put it better myself, there were no naked women. I reckon Potts has been over–doing it. All work and no play and the brain starts to go funny. You start imaging things. Seen it all before – and then... *(Slurps his beer.)*

GEORGE And then?

DAWSON It was when he talked about tinkling bells that I sussed him out...

GEORGE Did you say – bells?

(GEORGE suddenly becomes aware of the bells round his leg. Tries to remove and hide them, coughing to mask the sound of the bells.)

DAWSON That's right. *(Looking around)* Er, did you hear something then?

GEORGE Like – what, Sarge?

DAWSON Bells. Tinkling bells.

GEORGE No, Sarge. Not a thing.

DAWSON It all must be getting to me.

(GEORGE coughs more loudly.)

DAWSON Nasty cough you've got there, George. If it wasn't out of hours I'd recommend some liquid lubricant.

GEORGE I'll survive, Sarge. Er, down at the cricket field, did you notice anything – suspicious? *(He has managed to rid himself of the bells and hide them behind the bar.)*

DAWSON Only Potts. He had on a huge dressing gown that made him look like a bell tent. We had a look around but there was nothing. *(Thinks)* Ah, but there was a woman.

GEORGE You mean – one of those naked women? By heck, I would have liked to have met her.

DAWSON No such luck, lad. This one was fully clothed – what's more she was a witness...

GEORGE A witness. You mean – someone – saw? But who?

DAWSON That lass of yours, what's her name? Mary?

GEORGE Mary! *(Anxious)* And what did she have to say?

DAWSON That she was out walking and confirmed it.

GEORGE; She confirmed – what, Sarge?

DAWSON That there was nothing, not even a rabbit. Said it was as quiet as the grave.

GEORGE *(heaves a big sigh of relief.)* The grave, eh. And no naked women? But how did Potts know about these naked women?

DAWSON Claims this brass band woke him up, looked out and there they were – cavorting, naked. There was nothing when I got there. I reckon he'd been on the sauce – was pulling the wool over my eyes when he claimed there was a brass band. I ask you, how many is there in a band. Twenty – thirty? That number doesn't disappear into thin air. And where would they go? Holes in the ground?

GEORGE Maybe they were beamed up – by a flying saucer.

DAWSON You don't believe that crap do you? I reckon he'd been over–doing it. Personally, I've always stayed well clear of overwork; it hasn't done me any harm.

GEORGE Anyone can see that. I mean – you're a fine figure of a man, Alf.

DAWSON Good of you to say so, George. And talking of crap, did I ever tell you how I once came across a bloke on the Yorkshire moors one night. Two o'clock in the morning and there he was, stark bollock naked. *(He slurps his beer.)* Good drop of ale, George, and another one to go.

GEORGE Er, yes. But this bloke – starkers – you said...

DAWSON Him? Silly idiot tried to tell me he was Hannibal driving his elephants and camels over the hills to invade Lancashire. *(Pause)* But I wasn't having any. Takes a good one to fool me.

GEORGE You sussed him out then?

DAWSON Didn't take much. *(Pause)* He was going the wrong direction for Lancashire!

GEORGE And he was naked?

DAWSON Except for a flat cap and wellies. At least he had the sense to wear the wellies. I mean, would you fancy walking barefoot behind elephants and camels in the dark? Never know what they're leaving behind, do you? *(Pause)* Right lad. Time to take a notes. *(Takes out a notebook – licks pencil stub – writes.)* O two hundred. Single–handed investigated two suspicious packages rear of the Cobblers. Hint of bravery there, lad. Go down well with the Super. Packages found to be – harmless and dealt with in the appropriate manner. Now where's that other pint?

BLACKOUT

MUSIC

End of Scene 3.

ALL BALLS AND ASHES

ACT 11.

Scene 4.

The Cloggers Arms, the next evening. MARY and GEORGE are behind the bar. FRANK and ELI enter.

FRANK	See you are back with us, then Mary. Feeling better? The night air did you good?
MARY	Oh yes. Seems it did us all a bit of good. So, what's it to be, the usual?
GEORGE	Er, I'll get them, Mary. *(He pulls two pints.)*
ELI	You seem remarkably cheerful, lass.
MARY	Oh, I am and for good reason. You'll never believe it – *(with sarcasm)* – after all these years – oh, what a surprise – George ups and gives me a pay rise...
FRANK	He did? Now that's not like George. Business must be good.
MARY	Maybe it was for something else, eh?
ELI	Like what?
MARY	Well, actually, we had a little discussion before you arrived. One that just might have involved someone disturbing Freda. The poor love could have had a heart attack. Oh, and something about Seth's ashes and a certain cricket field? And I do feel so guilty about the little white lie I told Sergeant Dawson. Maybe I should go to church and confess my sin. Or perhaps I should go to Dawson and tell him all that I saw and heard.

FRANK *(aghast)* You mean – you know…?

ELI *(panicking)* I shall deny everything..

MARY Think on it, lads.

(GEORGE takes the two pints over to the table and motions FRANK and ELI over.)

GEORGE Am I glad to see you.

ELI Oh, it'll be cash, George, don't worry.

GEORGE Nay, it's not that.

MARY Er, I reckon they'll be – on the house – don't you, George?

GEORGE *(chokes then reluctantly)* Aye, well – maybe so. I take it Mary has told you her news?

FRANK Aye, and we think it's very generous of you. But you said you were glad to see us, George. It wasn't to give us pints on the house?

GEORGE Something else has come up. But first of all, Eli, you've had a visitor. You'll never guess who. Asked for you by name. Be back in a minute, she said…

ELI She! You mean a woman and asking for me? Fancy, a woman asking for me. *(He preens himself.)* So who's the lucky lady?

(As GEORGE opens his mouth, MARIGOLD enters. ELI beams expectantly.)

ELI *(whispering to others)* Marigold Potts, the bank manager's wife? What would she want with me?

GEORGE No, not her. It was…

(Enter ARNOLD POTTS.)

Hey, up. This could be trouble. I'd best see what he wants. And what can I get you and your lady, Mr Potts?

POTTS I would like a double scotch – no ice – and my good lady would like something a little less alcoholic and even less expensive.

MARY I'll get these, George.

GEORGE We don't often see you in here, Mr Potts. There's a darts match later, if you feel like throwing an arrow or two? Then of course, for the ladies there's always tombola. Perhaps Mrs Potts would like to...

MARIGOLD Er, and what do I do with this Tom Bola fellow?

POTTS I think it's a game, my dear...

MARIGOLD With someone called – Tom? That sounds like it could be fun... *(She accepts two drinks from MARY.)*

POTTS I don't think so, Marigold. *(To GEORGE)* Actually, we're not here to socialise, landlord. I am here for your support.

GEORGE Don't tell me – you're putting up for the council?

POTTS No, this is a matter more serious than politics. I'm looking for volunteers.

GEORGE To do what, Mr Potts?

MARIGOLD Arnold has uncovered...

POTTS *(cutting in.)* Hush, woman! *(Looks around to see he is not being overheard.)* Now, I don't wish to alarm you, landlord, but it seems this village has a problem with vandals. Could be some form of fertility sect. You know, sex and depravity and all that.

GEORGE *(loudly)* Gerraway! Sex! Here in Greenbridge?

(Everyone looks up in surprise.)

MARIGOLD Yes, sex! Isn't it exciting – Arnold thinks...

POTTS *(irritable)* Shush woman! I'll also trouble you to keep your voice down, landlord. And yes, here in Greenbridge. Once they get a foot in, my man, take my word it's the devil's own job to whittle them out.

GEORGE You've had experience of this sex?

POTTS Not – exactly. But I'm aware the place could be taken over. The village a den of iniquity. So, I want to form a sort of vigilante group to tackle them. With me in charge, of course.

GEORGE To keep them out or to keep them in?

POTTS Why, out of course. And with that intention, I would like to call a meeting here, if I may – meanwhile, not a word, eh, about?

GEORGE Sex and depravity? Sounds too good an opportunity to miss.

POTTS Good man, I knew I could count on you. Until the meeting, then. Right, drink up and come along, Marigold.

MARIGOLD Oh, but I haven't played with Tom!

(They exit. As they do so FREDA appears at the door, where she hesitates, looking for ELI. She is tight-lipped, grim-faced and has a carrier bag.)

GEORGE *(crosses to ELI'S table.)* I'm rushed off my feet. And she's here, Eli. Your date has arrived.

ELI *(sees FREDA heading towards him.)* Oh, Lord. I think we've been rumbled. I'm off.

(ELI heads towards the exit, closely followed by FRANK.)

FREDA *(barring their way)* And just where do you think you're going, Eli Cruickshanks? Sit yourself down , I've got summat to discuss with you.

(ELI obediently sits. FRANK is trying to slip out behind her.)

FREDA *(over her shoulder)* You too, Frank Bottomley. Your mate is going to need support.

(FRANK comes to an abrupt halt – then sheepishly returns and sits.)

Now we are all sitting comfortable and cosy, I thought you can throw a little light on a mystery that's beyond me.

FRANK What might that be, Freda? I'm not much good at mysteries, puzzles and such like. I'm more of a creative creature.

FREDA Really? I seem to have missed that stage of your evolution. But I'm sure you'll like this one. It comes with clues and the first one is in this bag. Here you are – I would like to know how this – thing – *(Pulls the tin hat from the carrier bag and thumps it on the table)* got under – my bed?

ELI A tin hat! Is that all?

FREDA What do you mean – is that all? What else would there be under there – the full bloody uniform? A whole battalion of Light Infantry? Like I said, this was under my bed this morning. I went for – well, never mind how I found it. But there it was grinning at me, like a great open mouth waiting to take a bite out of me. And don't deny it's yours, Eli Cruickshanks.

ELI But I do. I deny everything…

FREDA *(cutting in.)* Everything? That's a bit difficult seeing as how it's got you name on it as plain as day. Eli – Adelaide –

Cruickshanks!

(At the name "Adelaide" FRANK sits up and his jaw drops.)

FRANK Adelaide? You never said...

ELI It were Mum. She was – sort of – familiar – with this bloke from Australia, reckoned she had a thing about kangaroos and wanted a girl...

FREDA *(cutting in)* Wanted a girl, eh? If you ask me, she got one. So you admit this is yours. But the really big question is – how did it get under my bed?

ELI I'm admitting nothing.

FRANK Under your bed, you say? Perhaps it was – planted? Maybe Eli's being framed.

FREDA Framed? By whom?

FRANK Well, there's Scotland Yard. FBI. CIA.

ELI Not forgetting Interflora.

FREDA And what would he be framed for – stupidity?

FRANK Do you think Seth might have borrowed it.

FREDA Why would Seth want a tin hat?

ELI Protection?

FREDA From whom? There's only me. I admit I had a funny do last night, with all sorts of strange goings on. At first I thought it was summat I might have eaten. Maybe overdone the pickled onions. But it weren't that. When I couldn't sleep this thing turns up. So, have you any bright ideas?

(FREDA waits – there are no answers only silence – the men hide their faces in their pints.)

FREDA I can see I'm not going to get any change out of you two, so you'd best have it back. I reckon you've more need of it than me – especially if I find out what's really been going on.

(FREDA flounces out, leaving FRANK and ELI staring at one another. They are joined by GEORGE.)

GEORGE I reckon you got off lightly, lads.

ELI Call that getting off light? Freda can bear a grudge until the next millennium!

GEORGE You survived didn't you?

FRANK Do you reckon she knows?

GEORGE Maybe – maybe not.

(ELI is staring at the helmet.)

ELI This helmet – under the bed. You don't think – you know – in the dark –she – used it?

(They peer long and hard into the helmet.)

FRANK Dunno. Near enough the right shape, the right place under the bed.

MARY *(approaching)* Seems your little secret is destined not to be a secret for much longer. Oh, by the way, George. Have you told them about that chap from the council?

FRANK What chap from what council?

MARY Said something about the cricket match. Too technical for me, I'm only a woman. George will explain.

(MARY retires behind the bar. GEORGE sits between FRANK and ELI.)

GEORGE Some daft pillock came. Said he was from the council. He spots the match poster and talks about cricket. Then he says a funny thing..

ELI — That was?

GEORGE — About it being strange that a cricket match could be played in two counties at the same time.

FRANK — Two counties! How much had he had to drink?

GEORGE — One lemonade shandy – with a straw, tight sod. He came in stone cold sober and went out even more sober.

ELI — So what was he on about?

GEORGE — I'm coming to that. You remember some officials came round at the back end of last year. Said they were straightening out kinks?

FRANK — What kinks?

GEORGE — In the boundaries, between Yorkshire and Lancashire...

FRANK — If there are any kinks, they're bound to be on the Lancashire side...

GEORGE — Steady on, lad. My mother was born in Lancashire. I was conceived in Lancashire.

FRANK — We all have a cross to bear, George.

GEORGE — You're putting your credit in jeopardy, Frank.

ELI — Never mind the credit. What about these kinks?

GEORGE — Well, it seems there were a few on our side and they re–aligned them, but now it seems the boundary runs straight through the middle of the ground.

(Baffled silence.)

Don't you see, lads. Half the ground is in Yorkshire...

(Throws one arm left nearly hitting ELI.) The other half – is in Lancashire. *(Throws out other arm nearly decapitating FRANK.)*

FRANK Doesn't mean a thing to me.

ELI Ahhh! But it does if you're Yorkshire born – like Seth.

GEORGE That's right, Eli. Now–you tell me... *(He checks to see they are not being overheard – then lowers his voice.)* you tell me – where did we scatter Seth's ashes?

FRANK Difficult to say. We only had the moon to go on.

GEORGE That's exactly right, so?

(The other two are stumped. ELI is the first to cotton on.)

ELI Hell fire! Are you saying we might have scattered Seth in the wrong county?

GEORGE Got it in one, Eli.

FRANK Seth – in Lancashire? Well, we can't leave him there. Can we?

BLACKOUT.

End of Scene 4.

ALL BALLS AND ASHES

ACT 11.

Scene 5.

Night. The cricket field. As the lights come up (partially) GEORGE, FRANK and ELI are on their hands and knees with torhces and dustpans and brushes, searching for and trying to gather up Seth's ashes. They keep bumping into each other and grumbling. Eventually they get to their feet.

GEORGE Hopeless, could be here all night. You organised it Frank. Where do you think Seth is?

FRANK How the hell should I know? All I know is – things were going well until the Vicar arrived. I bet even Seth doesn't know where he is. What say you, Eli?

ELI Not guilty! I have an alibi, seeing to the brass band. You were dealing with the ashes.

(FRANK gets back to his hands and knees poking and probing. The others also start looking again then ELI makes a noise indicating that he has found something.)

GEORGE Got something, Eli?

ELI *(ELI briefly inspects what he is holding)* Yes, a handful of bloody rabbit droppings. *(Holds his hand out)* They say rabbits spend half their lives having sex. I reckon the other half is spent crapping.

(ELI tosses the handful into the audience. They resume the search. With their backsides to the audience they are unaware the VICAR has entered. He backs onto the stage

observing the sky through his telescope. He takes out a hip flask and takes a quick slurp. As he puts the flask away, he turns and is confronted by three backsides. He watches for a moment.)

VICAR Hello, lads. Another ancient ceremony. What is it this time, worm–charming?

(Startled, the three jump to their feet.)

FRANK Must you do that, Vicar? Fair put the wind up us...

VICAR I thought it a fair question. Why are you on your hands and knees? If it wasn't for the fact you are facing the wrong direction, I might have thought you were praying to Mecca!

ELI To tell you the truth, Vicar, it's the bone meal that you – I mean we – scattered the other night. Seems we put it in the wrong spot. Won't do much good where it is.

VICAR Really? But, we put it on the grass – didn't we?

FRANK Yes, Vicar. But you see, there's grass and there's grass. It needs to be on the wicket, that's the bit down the middle.

GEORGE Eli thought we'd cracked it. But it turned out to be a load of rabbit sh...

FRANK *(cutting in)* Doodah.

(ELI has resumed searching. He has found something.)

ELI Hang about! I've got something...

GEORGE Not more...

ELI *(cutting in)* No, this time I reckon I've struck bone meal. And there's more. The problem is – how are we going to get it up? I mean, those brushes are no good.

FRANK I think I have it. Why don't we use – a vacuum cleaner?

GEORGE Brilliant! Good thinking, Frank. Trust you to come up with a solution.

FRANK Aye. Not bad for a Yorkshire lad, eh?

VICAR Vacuum cleaner? Er, no lads. Where's your power? The nearest electric point must be a quarter of mile away.

ELI Now that is a problem. Why couldn't you think of that, Frank?

VICAR I have a divine thought. We could do it without electricity. By using another power.

GEORGE You're going to have us kneel down and call upon the Almighty. Well, I'm game.

(GEORGE kneels – others follow suit. They reverently put their hands together in prayer.)

VICAR No, not quite like that, lads, the solution is in the vicarage. Meanwhile, I'll leave you to your searching and perhaps this might help. Toodle pip.

(The VICAR hands GEORGE the telescope and exits. GEORGE puts it to his eye – wrong way round. FRANK takes it off him – turns it around and hands it back. All try the telescope in turn. The VICAR re–enters. He is carrying a carpet sweeper.)

VICAR The solution, gentlemen.Good for picking up confetti after a wedding with the added bonus of not disturbing those who shall we say are – sleeping in the graveyard.

ELI For man of the cloth, Vicar, you're a bloody genius. Er, begging your pardon.

VICAR In such a time of crisis you are forgiven. I will truly pray for you my son. So, would you like me to do the honours? Where, about here – or maybe there?

FRANK Where you are standing will do fine, Vicar. If it's as good as you say, a few careful sweeps should do it.

(The VICAR makes deft sweeps. The others watch, then go into a burst of the 'Shake and Vac' TV advert, to the VICAR'S annoyance. GEORGE and ELI exit leaving the VICAR to empty the carpet sweeper's contents into the coffee tin held by FRANK.)

FRANK That will do nicely, Vicar. Thank you. And God bless you.

(FRANK exits, leaving a puzzled VICAR staring after him.)

VICAR The Lord works in mysterious ways. There go three more converts.

(Before he can leave FREDA enters. She is tearful and cradling Seth's urn.)

VICAR Goodness me, I'm surprised to see you out at this time of night, Mrs Hegginbotham.

FREDA Oh, it's you, Vicar. Nice to see someone sensible. Never know who you might bump into in the dark, or what they might be up to.

VICAR That is very true, my dear. But, is everything all right, you look, well…troubled?

FREDA Yes, Vicar. I am. But it's Seth, you see.

VICAR Seth? But I thought he was beyond being troubled.

FREDA Oh, I'm not so sure about that. I've had a couple of bad nights, Vicar. Terrible nightmares… I think I want exorcising. *(The VICAR looks alarmed)* I could swear I had the devil in my bedroom the other night. A visit from old Nick himself...

VICAR The devil – Satan! Goodness me, that is not good...

(Visibly shaken he takes out his flask and takes a quick sip unseen by FREDA.)

FREDA You're telling me. But it gets worse, Vicar.

VICAR Worse? Oh, dear. *(Nervously looks all around him, then takes another quick slurp.)*

FREDA You see, what happened fair put the wind up me. Couldn't sleep. I mean – it's not every night you get a visit from the devil – and then there was that tin hat thing...

VICAR *(cutting in.)* You mean the devil was wearing – a tin hat?

FREDA Oh, no, it was under my bed, see. How it got there I cannot think...

VICAR Most intriguing. Perhaps if you sit and tell me all.

(They sit on a bench.VICAR lays down the carpet sweeper and telescope, takes out the hip flask. VICAR sees FREDA eyeing the flask.)

VICAR Er, medication –for the throat, my dear. Sermons can be so hard on the voice.

FREDA First medication I've heard of that comes out of a hip flask. Maybe I should have a word with my chemist.

VICAR Well, there is a little something added.

FREDA Something added, eh?

VICAR Er, yes. Why don't you try some. It's my own special home brew and this month was extra special. The something added I can certainly recommend.

FREDA Oh, if it's alcohol – I couldn't – I mean, I shouldn't, Vicar.

VICAR Oh, good. I mean –it's only harmless altar wine, my dear. Comes with the Lord's blessing.

FREDA Really? In that case. *(She takes a cautious swig. Likes it and takes bigger gulp.)* By heck, Vicar. Never had altar wine like that. Strong – but nice. Yes, very nice.

(VICAR has to fight to get the flask back.)

VICAR For some, an acquired taste, my dear.

(FREDA wrestles back the flask.)

FREDA Oh, I've acquired a taste for it alright, Reverend.

(Takes another swig. VICAR hastily takes the flask away. It will be snatched back and forth.)

VICAR *(trying to change the subject)* Now – that thing – under your bed?

FREDA Thing? Oh, yes. Something woke me up in the middle of the night; when I put the light on there it was, a tin hat slowly rising up out of no–where. And beneath it there was this – devil thing. It popped out of no–where, all shouting with an ugly, silly green face – and...

VICAR Did you say – ugly green face?

FREDA I did. Why? Don't tell me green's your favourite colour.

VICAR Oh, no. Only that – ugly and green seems to be in fashion at the moment.

FREDA I do hope not, Vicar.

VICAR And what happened next?

FREDA Well, I know it sounds daft, but I swear that this – thing, smiled at me. Sort of showed its teeth. I thought it was going to bite me and I went all funny like.

VICAR Oh, dear. And then?

FREDA I think I fainted. When I came round it had gone and it was as quiet as the grave. Later I got to thinking maybe it was Seth come to punish me.

VICAR Punish you? Why would your late husband want to do that?

FREDA Er, funny. I seem to have forgotten. Perhaps another wee sip of that medication?

(Flask is snatched before the VICAR can stop her. FREDA takes large gulp and hangs onto the flask.)

FREDA Ah, that's much better. Now where was I? Oh, yes. With Seth spending so much time practising his cricket, playing dominoes and bird–watching, maybe I was a bit hard on him. Then when I looked, I saw the ashes had turned a funny colour and there was an odd smell – like coffee. Which was funny, cos' Seth never drank the stuff. So I reckon he was sending me a message.

VICAR A message?

FREDA Seems he wanted his ashes scattered over the cricket field, so I decided to bring them here. Thought he'd forgive me if I carried out his wishes.

VICAR A message from the other side. God moves in mysterious ways.

FREDA True, but talking of moving in mysterious ways. What are you doing in the middle of the night with a telescope and a carpet sweeper?

VICAR Actually, I'm beginning to wonder myself. Er, and these are Seth's ashes?

FREDA *(hiccups)* Yes, the very same.

VICAR In that case then, you could say God has led Seth, you and I along a golden path to enlightenment. So, shall we do the honourable thing and commit Seth's ashes to a last resting place?

(They stand. FREDA is noticeably unsteady – is supported by the VICAR. Seth's ashes are scattered to the accompaniment of the VICAR's prayer.)

VICAR Ashes to ashes. Dust to dust.

(There is rather a lot of ash. FREDA looks surprised.)

FREDA Eee, I didn't think there was that much of him.

(VICAR bangs on the urn one last time. The last remnants fall out.)

FREDA. After all that, it seems he was reluctant to leave me.

VICAR Love comes in many forms, my dear. And now Seth will be with our team in their hour of need

FREDA You know I feel much better now, Vicar. It's a long time since I felt so – uplifted. Like you said, God works in mysterious ways. He must be with us. Hic! Oops, sorry, Vicar. I don't know what's come over me…

(FREDA staggers – clearly showing the effects of the wine. The VICAR takes her arm at the same time neatly taking the flask.)

VICAR Perhaps I should escort you home, my dear.

FREDA I'll be alright, Vicar. Nice ceremony. We must do it again sometime. *(FREDA weaves her way out. VICAR takes another sip. To his disgust the flask is empty.)*

FREDA *(offstage)* Enjoyed the medication, Vicaaaaaa...

(Her voice abruptly tails off and there is the sound of a crash. VICAR rushes to tend to her. Stage briefly empty. Enter ARNOLD POTTS, bent double, wearing top coat, deer stalker and carrying a shotgun, he crosses the stage furtively looking right and left. Fails to see returning VICAR. They collide centre–stage, frightening each other and falling to the floor. They sit up, POTTS brings up the shotgun. VICAR brings up the telescope.)

POTTS GOTCHA! Up with your hands up, you varmit. I'll teach you to disturb my sleep.

(He sees the telescope, which he mistakes for a gun. At the same moment the VICAR sees the shot gun.)

VICAR and POTTS *(In unison.)* DON'T SHOOT! DON'T SHOOT!

VICAR *(starting to pray)*
'Our father, who art in heaven. Hallowed be….'

POTTS Vicar? Good grief, it is you! What on earth are you doing here at this time of night? I thought that you – Look, I'm terribly sorry old chap. *(His gun is still pointed at the VICAR.)*

VICAR MR POTTS! Will you take that instrument of the devil out of my face before you do some harm – to me!

POTTS What instrument of the devil? Oh, the gun. *(He lowers it.)* No need to panic. Damn thing isn't loaded anyway. But you still haven't answered my question. What are you doing here?

VICAR I ask you the same question. At least I've only got a

telescope, not a shotgun.

POTTS If you must know – there are vandals, Vicar. Performing fertility rites on our very doorstep...Hordes of them, they'll be coming by the thousand if we don't stop them.

VICAR You jest, sir.

POTTS I jest not, Vicar. Why I even had to involve the law in the early hours. Mind you, they were useless. Couldn't find a vandal if he or she jumped up and bit them on the arse. Er, begging your pardon, Vicar but may I ask what you are doing here?

VICAR Well, I was er, performing a certain – religious ceremony.

POTTS What! Not you too, Vicar?

VICAR What! Oh, good lord no. Just a service of comfort for a bereaved parishioner. So, having frightened the life out of me, what do you now intend doing?

POTTS To be truthful, if the pub wasn't closed, I'd have a double scotch.

VICAR Really? Well, I do confess I too feel in the need of some stimulant. *(Takes out flask)* But I'm afraid my flask is sadly depleted. However, I do have a reserve of a rather splendid altar wine back at the rectory. Perhaps you would like to join me?

POTTS Altar wine? You couldn't make it – whisky, old chap?

VICAR Ah, but this is altar wine with a difference. Some would say it's – rather uplifting.

POTTS Really? Well, that sounds interesting. The little lady has been safely tucked up in bed and won't be expecting me home for a little while, so – shall we?

(They exit together. FRANK and ELI enter.)

FRANK At last we've done the right thing by Seth and scattered him where he wanted to be. To be honest, I was glad to see the back of the old chap, I got a bit tired of lugging that coffee tin around.

ELI Yes. He'll be alright round the back of the pavilion. He may not be able to watch the match but at least we know he's definitely in Yorkshire soil.

(Sounds off–stage, someone is coming. FRANK and ELI duck out of sight. MARY enters stage right carrying a single rose. Halts centre stage.)

MARY Eeeh, Seth. I'm not sure where you've ended up, where exactly they put you. But I know your heart was always here where we spent time canoodling. Right sex pot you were, with more go in you than all the young village studs put together. If only your mates knew. *(She kisses the rose and lays it down.)* Sleep well, Hot Balls. Love you… *(MARY exits. GEORGE and ELI emerge shaking their heads.)*

FRANK Well, I'll go to the foot of our stairs…

ELI Who'd have thought it?

(More sounds of footsteps off–stage.)

FRANK Hey, up. There's someone else coming.

(They hide again. MARIGOLD enters carrying flowers which she lays down.)

MARIGOLD Ooooh, Hotballs – you old devil you! Dancing in the moonlight will never be the same.

(She pretends to waltz with an imaginary Seth for a moment, then blows a kiss and exits. FRANK and ELI emerge scratching their heads.)

FRANK That Eli – was…

ELI Marigold Potts – but how did she know?

(More footsteps. The two again duck behind the shrubbery. Enter DOLLY stage right. She too lays a flower, dabs her eyes. As she does so ELI jumps up.)

ELI *(strangled cry)* That's my wife Dolly!

(DOLLY doesn't hear. ELI is pulled down by FRANK.)

DOLLY I don't know how we kept it a secret for so long, Seth. Poor Eli, if only he knew what was going on whilst he snored his little head off. I promise – no–one will ever know.

(DOLLY blows a kiss and exits. Sound of more footsteps. VERA enters also carrying flowers. It is FRANK's turn to jump up.)

FRANK *(aghast)* Vera?

(ELI pulls him down. VERA doesn't notice anything. She dabs her eyes.)

VERA Hmm, wonder where the other flowers came from? Probably from his pals. That's nice. But – village life will never be the same without those sneaked cuddles behind the pavilion, lad. Love you.

(She exits. FRANK and ELI emerge.)

FRANK Bloody hell. Would you believe it? How many more are there?

ELI I'm not counting and I'm not taking any bets. *(Pause)* But I'll tell you this, Frank, I reckon I could quite take to this bird–watching lark.

FRANK You've got to give Seth his due. I always thought he was talking about cricket when he went on about the happy times spent here...

ELI And I thought the lasses were cricket fans when they called him, 'Hot–balls'!

(They leave the centre stage – one left, one right. Pause briefly – having the same thoughts. Then return to centre stage and come together.)

FRANK Let's give it one last time for Seth.

FRANK and ELI *(In unison)* HOT BALLS!!

(BLACKOUT. The shout of "HOT BALLS" echoes several times in the darkness. MUSIC.)

THE END.

FURNITURE LIST

The Cloggers Arms:	Bar, with beer pumps; small table; three wooden chairs.
FREDA's house:	An armchair; a two seater sofa; a side table.
FREDA's house (exterior)	A 'coal chute'.
Jasper's Bottom:	The side of a shed (with cricket scoreboard); a wooden bench; some 'shrubbery'.
POTT's house:	a table with a telephone and telephone books.

PROPERTY LIST

Page 1	pint of beer, dominoes (FRANK)
	Racing paper (GEORGE)
	Dishcloth (MARY)
Page 2	flat cap (ELI)
Page 4	pint glasses, notebook (on or behind the bar)
Page 5	coat (offstage, MARY)
Page 10	newspaper, urn of ashes (FREDA)
Page 18	glass cloth, pint glasses (GEORGE)
Page 21	coat (MARY)
Page 26	mop and bucket (MARY)
Page 31	balaclavas (FRANK and ELI) steel helmet (ELI) carrier bag containing large coffee tin (GEORGE)
Page 33	coin (FRANK)
Page 35	ancient bicycle and torch (DAWSON)
Page 37	notebook and pencil (DAWSON)
Page 39	coffee tin (FRANK)
Page 43	telescope, hip flask (VICAR) coffee tin, carrier bag containing Morris bells (2 sets), flowered hats (3) Morris sticks, small working CD player with Morris music in, handkerchiefs (3) (FRANK)
Page 46	pram containing boom box playing Black Dyke Mills band music (ELI)
Page 52	dressing gowns (POTTS and MARIGOLD)
Page 57	negligee (MARIGOLD)
Page 58	pint of beer (GEORGE)
Page 59	bells around leg (GEORGE)

Page 62	notebook and pencil (DAWSON)
Page 63	two pints of beer (GEORGE)
Page 65	glass of scotch and a glass of sherry (MARY)
Page 66	carrier bag containing steel helmet (FREDA)
Page 72	torches, dustpans and brushes (3) (FRANK, GEORGE and ELI) 'rabbit droppings' (suggest little balls of dark brown paper as they are thrown into the audience!) (ELI) telescope, hip flask (VICAR)
Page 74	carpet sweeper (VICAR)
Page 75	urn containing dust (FREDA)
Page 80	coat, deer stalker hat, shotgun (POTTS)
Page 82	single rose (MARY) flowers (MARIGOLD) flower (DOLLY) flowers (VERA)

LIGHTING AND EFFECTS PLOT

Start of play	*MUSIC, LIGHTS, interior day.*
Page 9	CUE: GEORGE: Best offer I've had all night...
	LIGHTS: Blackout.
	SFX: MUSIC, which plays until set is changed.
Page 10	*SFX: MUSIC fades.*
	LIGHTS: up to interior settings.
Page 17	CUE: FRANK: More like putting it on the slate...
	LIGHTS: Blackout.
	SFX: MUSIC, which plays until set is changed.
Page 18	*SFX: MUSIC fades.*
	LIGHTS: up to interior settings.
Page 25	CUE: GEORGE: He's buying a round!
	LIGHTS: Blackout.
	SFX: MUSIC, which plays until set is changed.
Page 26	*SFX: MUSIC fades.*
	LIGHTS: up to interior settings.
	CUE: VERA: – is George there?
	SFX: sound of bolts being drawn.
Page 30	CUE: DOLLY and VERA: Well, if you say so.
	LIGHTS: Blackout.
	SFX: MUSIC, which plays until set is changed.
Page 31	*SFX : MUSIC fades.*
	LIGHTS: up to moonlight setting.
	CUE: GEORGE: War zone? Don't be daft.
	SFX: Loud snoring.
Page 34	CUE: FRANK: I want some protection.

	SFX: After a pause, an owl hoots.
	CUE: ELI: Sounds like our man has made *contact...*
	SFX: sound of helmet hitting chamber pot.
Page 35	CUE: FREDA: Is that you Seth?
	LIGHTS: a light comes on in the window.
	CUE: FREDA screams.
	LIGHTS: Light in window goes out.
	SFX: A thud is heard, then sound of helmet hitting chamber pot again.
	CUE: GEORGE: I knew it would go wrong!
	SFX: Squeaking bicycle offstage and torch flashes.
Page 42	CUE: ELI: ...rank and number on it, that's why!
	LIGHTS: Blackout.
	SFX: MUSIC. Interval MUSIC. House lights.
Page 43	*SFX: MUSIC, which then fades.*
	LIGHTS: up to moonlight setting.
	SFX: Owl hooting.
Page 44	*SFX: FRANK switches on Morris music.*
Page 46	CUE: ELI: I'll come and join you.
	SFX: FRANK switches off Morris music.
	CUE: FRANK: Bring on the band!
	SFX: Black Dyke Mills band music offstage at loud volume.
Page 47	CUE: ELI: That is Black Dyke brass band, no less.
	SFX: VICAR switches off music.
Page 50	*SFX: VICAR turns on Morris music.*
Page 51	CUE: GEORGE: I bloody hope not!

	LIGHTS: Blackout.
	SFX: MUSIC continues but fades to background and plays until p.56.
Page 52	*LIGHTS: Spotlight on POTTS.*
Page 56	CUE: MARIGOLD: There is no need to shout...
	SFX: Stop Morris music.
Page 57	CUE: MARIGOLD: - a very sexy tango?
	LIGHTS: Slowly fade spotlight.
	SFX: Victor Sylvester tango music, which continues until set is changed.
Page 58	*SFX: MUSIC fades.*
	LIGHTS: up to interior setting.
	SFX: knock at the door, then bolts being drawn.
Page 62	CUE: DAWSON: Now, where's that other pint?
	LIGHTS: Blackout.
	SFX: MUSIC, which plays until set is changed.
Page 63	*SFX: Music fades.*
	LIGHTS: up to interior setting.
Page 71	CUE: FRANK: Well, we can't leave him there, can we?
	LIGHTS: Blackout.
	SFX: MUSIC, which plays until set is changed.
Page 72	*SFX: MUSIC fades.*
	LIGHTS: up to moonlight setting.
Page 84	CUE: FRANK: Let's give it one last time for Seth.
	SFX: HOT BALLS (echoes several times.)
	LIGHTS: Blackout.
	SFX: MUSIC for curtain calls.

A SUGGESTED BASIC SET

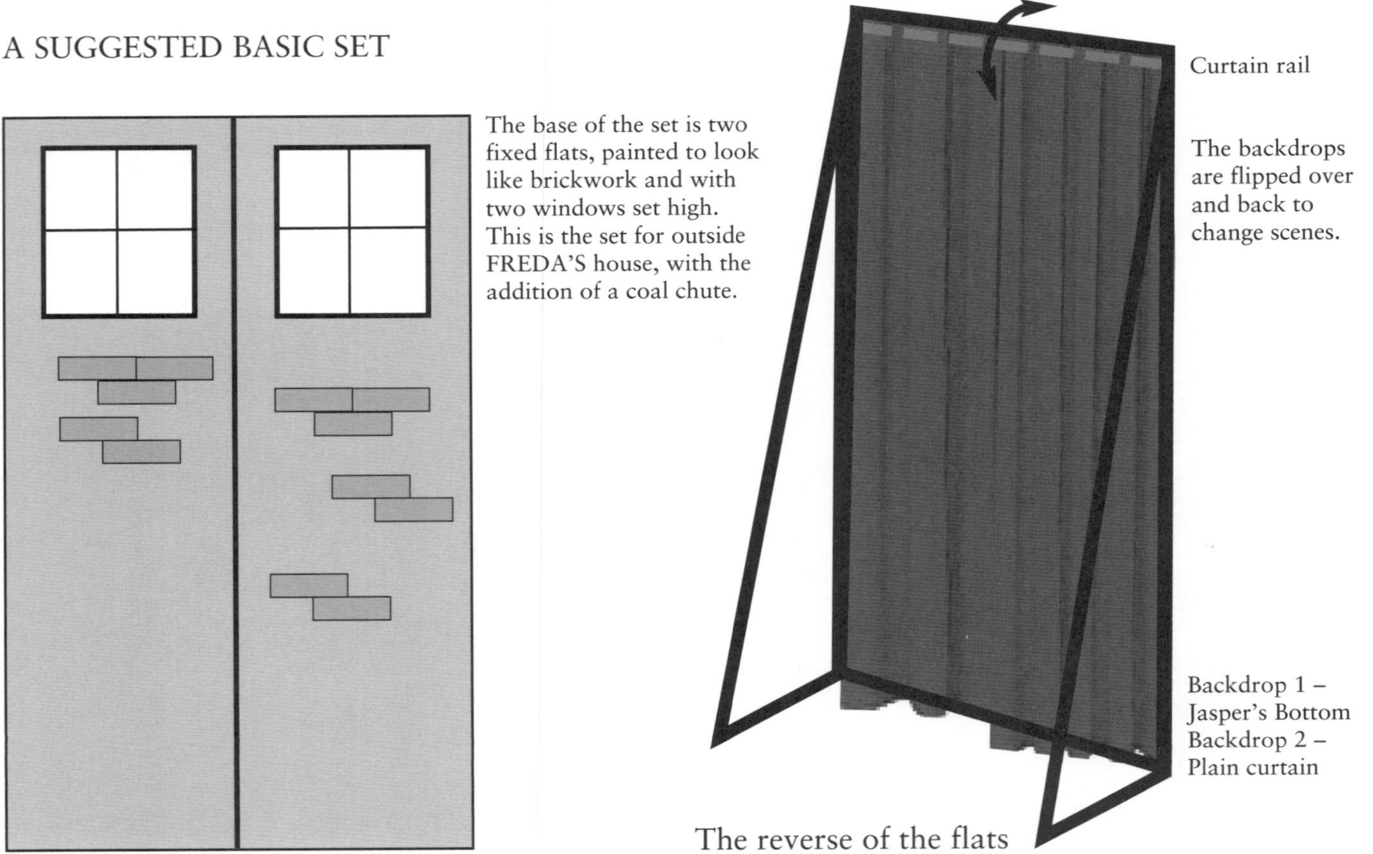

The reverse of the flats

THE VERSATILE BOXES (IN LIGHTWEIGHT WOOD)

Each box should be the width of one flat

At least 1m high

The Cloggers Arms bar – made up of two boxes with wood panel effect front.

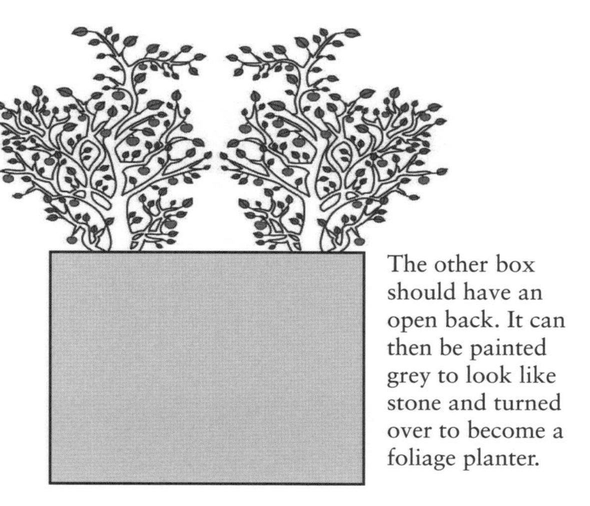

The other box should have an open back. It can then be painted grey to look like stone and turned over to become a foliage planter.

Deep enough for a man to hide in.

One of the boxes has a hinged back so it can be laid on its front and become the coal chute. The sides and hinged top should be painted to look like planks.

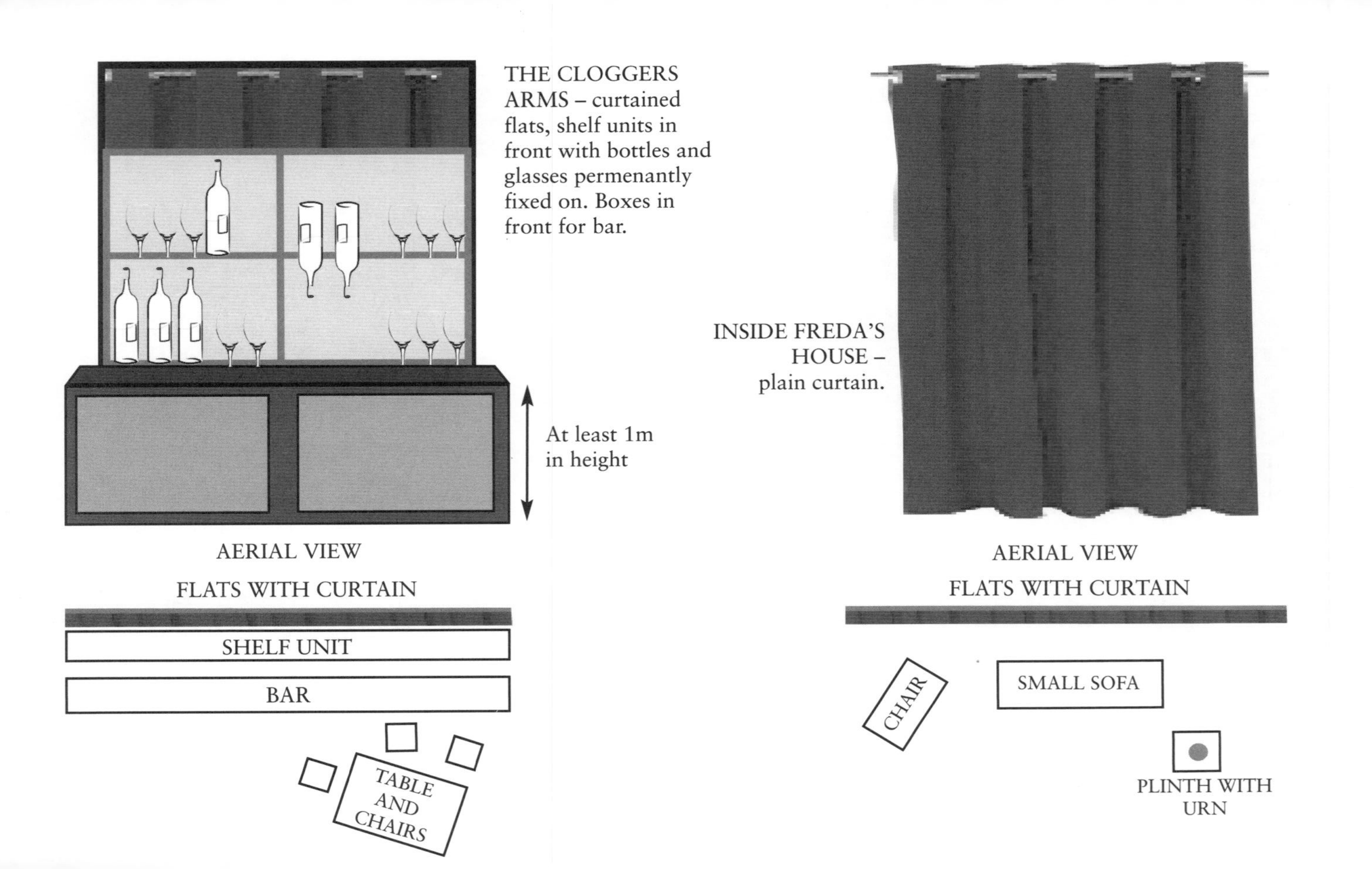
THE CLOGGERS ARMS – curtained flats, shelf units in front with bottles and glasses permenantly fixed on. Boxes in front for bar.
At least 1m in height
AERIAL VIEW
FLATS WITH CURTAIN
SHELF UNIT
BAR
TABLE AND CHAIRS
INSIDE FREDA'S HOUSE – plain curtain.
AERIAL VIEW
FLATS WITH CURTAIN
CHAIR
SMALL SOFA
PLINTH WITH URN

OUTSIDE FREDA'S HOUSE

AERIAL VIEW

FLATS

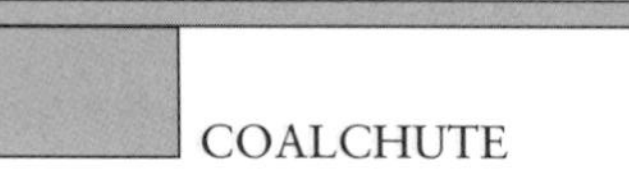

JASPER'S BOTTOM – canvas with mock shiplap and scoreboard.

AERIAL VIEW

FLATS